This book is dedicated to all my family, those who came before me and to those who come after me.

Drawings by Caitriona O'Leary
notesfrom6b.wordpress.com

Layout and graphic design by Toni Ricart
www.multistudio.com

Published by Anthony Griffin

Printed by CreateSpace, An Amazon.com Company

Available from Amazon.com, CreateSpace.com,
and other retail outlets

The G Spot
A Book About Squash

Tony Griffin

What is the G Spot?.. 8

Where is the G Spot?..9

Starting at the beginning, the Grip 11

Racket preparation.. 12

Racket movement and hitting the ball........................14

Shots 19

       Straight and crosscourt drives 19

       Drives 22

       Straight drives 23

       Straight drive from midcourt................................ 29

       Crosscourt drives from the midcourt area 30

       Driving from the back of the court 31

       Serve 32

       Return of serve 34

       Boast 35

       Reverse angle boast 41

       Skid boast 42

       Drop shot 43

       Drop shot from the front of the court 48

       Crosscourt drop shots 48

       Volleys 50

       Overhead forehand volley 51

       Overhead backhand volley 54

       Overhead volley kill 55

       Straight volley kill shots 56

       Crosscourt volley nick shots 56

       Overhead dying length volley 57

       Volley drop shot 58

       Lob 60

Practice routines 63

Tactics 84

Mental fitness 93

Physical Fitness 100

A little bit about me 107

Acknowledgements 113

Testimonials 115

6

I will start by answering the obvious question, why is a book about squash titled 'The G Spot'? Many years ago when I first thought about putting my ideas and experiences from inside a squash court into a book, the search for an appropriate title had me a bit baffled. Ideas like 'The Right Place', 'The Perfect Place', 'The Good Place', 'The Perfect Spot', 'The Soft Spot', 'The Sweet Spot', 'The Right Spot', 'Getting to the Comfort Zone' and many others came to mind. None of them seemed right. Then, 'The G Spot' came to me and it made me smile. While smiling about this possible title for my collection of ideas, 'G' words started coming to mind as possible explanations or justifications for a title that may have other connotations. Words like my surname Griffin or Good, or Gift or even God but, in the end, the title 'The G Spot—A Book About Squash' simply made me smile.

Squash is about putting a lot of small details together. Many of these details in themselves are often not considered to be overly important. Yet, to do well in squash, the maximum number of these details need to be put together to improve. As more time is spent on the squash court practicing and playing we gradually coordinate and incorporate more and more of these details into our game. In this process we create habits that often become a subconscious part of the way we play. In this book I will try and talk about some of these details and how they are interrelated. I have noticed that the more conscious we become of these details, how they are put together and kept together during the course of points, games and matches will help us improve and become more consistent in our game.

It is important to remember that your body needs time to evolve and incorporate new habits. You build them with practice and develop an awareness of what you are asking your body and mind to do. New habits are acquired over time, they are also lost over time if you are not working on them. Once you have developed a new habit, the next step is to add new objectives. Remember that to improve you need to develop technical, tactical, physical and psychological habits. Try not to focus on any single area, they are all interrelated and need work. It is a never ending and on-going process.

What is the 'G Spot'?

The G Spot is that elusive spot. The point where everything feels right and the ball goes exactly where you want it to go. This is because you have connected the racket and ball at exactly the right spot, the G Spot.

The problem with the G Spot is that you cannot just hit on it whenever you want or need to. To get to the G Spot consistently you must unify and combine a whole series of factors like moving to the ball, having correct racket movement and body position. In turn, each one of these components involve a whole series of details that must be understood and put into practice. You also need to understand the interrelationship of all these details, for example, if your racket movement is right but body position is not, your chances of hitting from the G Spot will be limited to say the least. Adding to the mix the fact that squash is played at a very high speed further complicates your chances of hitting the ball from the G Spot.

In a more general context, I think every profession or sport has its G Spot. To get to it, or see it, requires a detailed understanding of all the small things that need to be put together and how each one is interrelated. With this understanding, the activity can be successful at ever increasing and higher levels.

Without really knowing in-depth any of the martial arts that have evolved over centuries in Asian countries, I have always been impressed and fascinated by their ability to take almost anyone to a very high level of competence. They do this by following a step-by-step process that starts from zero and only permits the individual to move on to the next level once they have mastered their current level. I also like the way they develop natural and fluid movements, understanding the most efficient flows of energy through their bodies and how it can be best used.

This radically contrasts with how we work in the western world, where we are given a ball of some description, often at a young age, and we just start to play.

Where is the G Spot?

The G Spot is the place where your body naturally and instinctively hits the ball from. Our forehand and backhand racket swings are basically the same arm movements that, put simply, move in opposite directions. Therefore it stands to reason that the point of impact of the racket with the ball should be the same spot in respect of our body.

The G Spot is perpendicular to your shoulders and in line with your racket arm or shoulder. It is the same spot for both forehand and backhand.

Forehand and backhand G Spots

In reality, the G Spot is where we hit the ball from naturally and instinctively but, because squash is so fast, we generally are not conscious of the specific point of impact. The ball is moving, our body is moving to the ball and our racket is moving, therefore our instincts take over and we naturally hit the ball from the right place. When the ball does not go where we want it to, it is because, for some reason, we have not connected at the G Spot.

What helped me realise that the G Spot is in front of the shoulder of your racket arm, was observing the way we hit the ball during many years of playing and coaching squash. I saw that, often on the forehand side, some players tend to hit the ball well past the top of the bounce and sometimes even let the ball get close to the floor before striking it, whereas this seldom happens on the backhand side. This lead me to think that on the forehand we instinctively and subconsciously wait for the ball to get to the G Spot so that we can hit it comfortably.

This may explain why squash matches are played slightly more on the backhand side. It appears to be naturally easier to play a straight shot on the backhand side.

To start with, whether or not you have hit the ball from the G Spot is more noticeable when you are playing a shot that requires precision for example drop shots, kill shots or nicks. I believe that if the ball goes too high it is because the point of impact is behind the G Spot and if it goes too low or down (hitting the tin) then the point of impact is in front of the G Spot.

It is instantly noticeable in precision shots if the ball was not hit from the right spot. Yet it is important to hit the ball from the G Spot every time so that all the energy and effort we put into the shot is transferred to the ball. This will help gain consistency, which is extremely important in our sport. Squash is often a game of attrition with both players playing a high number of shots in each rally. You often only see the results of consistently hitting the ball well after 15 to 20 minutes of play, or even a lot longer time.

So if you hit the ball from the same spot in relation to your body it will go to where you want it to almost every time. To be able to do this you need to understand and control the way you move to the ball, and then your racket movement, so that you hit the ball at the G Spot. We will now start looking at these movements in detail, see how they are interrelated and discuss how to put them all together.

Starting at the beginning, the Grip

The way you hold the racket will condition your future in squash. If it is not correct it will limit the level that you are able to attain. It may also limit the time you play squash, as often those who do not hold the racket correctly become frustrated and stop playing. I recently attended a small veterans' tournament where I noted that all the players held their racket correctly.

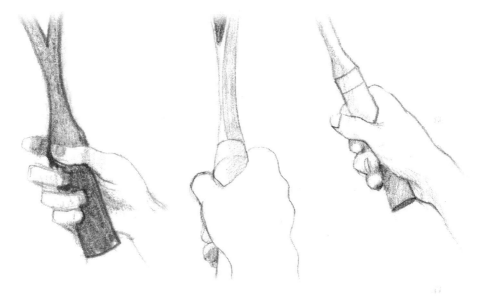

The grip

The correct grip is one that allows us to hit the ball with an open racket face on both the forehand and backhand sides without changing how we hold the racket. The 'V' where your thumb meets your forefinger should be over the left-hand side (or corner) of the racket handle or grip for right-handers. This, at the same time, places your forefinger knuckle over the top right side (or corner) of the grip. For left-handers the 'V' where your thumb meets your forefinger should be over the right-hand side (or corner) of the grip. This, at the same time, places your forefinger knuckle over the top left side (or corner) of the grip. There are a few millimetres of tolerance according to where each individual feels most comfortable.

Your forefinger should also be slightly separated from the rest of your fingers. This gives a similar racket surface for hitting the ball from both the forehand and backhand sides of the court.

It is the same as how you would hold a hammer. Imagine hitting a nail with anything but the correct grip!

Racket preparation*

Ideally your racket should be stationary and in the starting point before you commence your swing to hit the ball. Given the speed of our sport this is easier said than done. Most players start their racket movement when they get to the ball or when it bounces in front of them. The ball bouncing seems to be the subconscious signal to our body that we need to start thinking about our racket and hitting the ball. Before this moment we are normally thinking (or worrying), principally, about getting to the ball. For this reason the process of preparing the racket often becomes part of the racket swing and there appears to be no definition between the racket preparation and the action of hitting the ball. I think this is completely understandable given the speed of squash. I was always told about the importance of having or getting your 'racket up' before hitting the ball. I have seen that this often means that the racket is basically stationary (which in itself is good) and vertical in the air in front of the shoulder.

"Racket up" backhand and forehand

*Ian Mckenzie, who I met when I arrived in London a million and two years ago, helped me to start seeing and defining the importance of racket preparation.

From this position the racket moves back until your upper arm is in line with the shoulder on the forehand, or on the backhand your upper arm and elbow are close to your body. Then the racket continues down behind the ball before hitting it. The direction (in part) and speed of the ball are defined during the downward movement to the ball so the racket movement from the 'up' position to the 'back' position means that your swing is a little longer and needs a little more time for the racket to get to the ball. For this reason I prefer to say 'racket back' rather than 'racket up'.

"Racket back" forehand and backhand

Therefore if you eliminate the 'up' position racket movement and use the 'back' position instead, you start the swing to the ball from the 'back' position and reduce or simplify the movement which will help to improve your accuracy. You also reduce the time you need to hit the ball, so when it comes back to you at high speed, or is in a difficult position, you will have more chance of returning the ball well.

If we look at a couple of other impact or precision sports you see that they use simple and precise preparation which helps them to develop a high level of accuracy. In archery they do not pull the arrow and string back and let it go as soon as it is in the prepared position. They have it prepared, they aim and then they let the arrow go.

In boxing or the martial arts they do not have their fists in front of their bodies while they are looking for the moment to throw a punch. They have their fists back and prepared. When they see the opportunity or moment to strike their opponents they punch forward to their target with one simple, but powerful movement.

Understanding and training yourself to have good, clear racket preparation will help you to hit the ball more consistently from the G Spot.

Racket movement and hitting the ball

When hitting the ball you are looking for a fluid, natural arm movement that ensures all the force or power you are putting into the swing is transferred into the ball.

Forehand

The first reference point is that your upper arm is in line with your shoulders behind your body and with your elbow bent. I have seen that the position of the forearm varies a lot from person to person and I think that everyone needs to look for the position they are most comfortable with. The objective is to hit the ball just below its centre.

Forearm movement

As we start the downward movement towards the ball, the racket moves down behind the ball and it falls behind the wrist. This is because of the natural forearm movement caused by the speed with which we are moving the racket forwards towards the ball.*

Racket prepared   Forehand G Spot

Forehand follow though

The moment that the wrist comes in line with the G Spot is when the racket face catches up and impacts with the ball. The face of the racket should be slightly open. From here the racket should be briefly moving in the direction you wish the ball to go. This is the moment you transfer the speed/power/effort from your swing into the ball, so if the racket is not moving through the ball in the direction you want it to go in, some of your effort is not passed into the ball (it is probably simple physics) resulting in the ball not going exactly where you wanted it to. The

*I became conscious of this part of the racket movement thanks to Geoff Hunt. He explained it in a clinic he gave in Antwerp, Belgium a million years ago, where I was fortunate enough to play an exhibition game with him.

racket should then continue upward with your wrist finishing up by your other shoulder. Your racket face should still be open when the movement is finished.

Backhand

The racket movement is in the same line as the forehand, but in the opposite direction. The starting point is with your upper arm and elbow close to your body and your hand at the height of your back shoulder. From here you start the downward movement of the racket towards the ball. As the racket moves down behind the ball, the racket again falls behind the wrist because of the natural forearm movement (just the same as it does on the forehand).

Racket prepared

Backhand G Spot

Backhand follow through

The moment that your wrist comes in line with the G Spot is when the racket face catches up and impacts with the ball. The face of the racket should again be slightly open. From here the racket should be briefly moving in the direction you wish the ball to go, and then rises to finish in a position that is similar to the starting point of the forehand. It is important for both forehand and backhand sides that your shoulders are in line with the direction you would like the ball to go in and they should move very little when you are hitting it.

Body position and feet

Imagine you draw a line through both your shoulders. This is the line that should give direction to the ball so you should try and maintain your shoulders in the same position while you are swinging the racket. Remember that when you are hitting the ball hard there will always be some shoulder movement. Your shoulder direction conditions your hip position and consequently your foot position. It could also be said the other way round; that your foot position conditions your hip and shoulder position. Be aware that your hip position also conditions and can help the position of your feet and shoulders.

All three positions are correct. What is really important is that you are conscious of all three; feet, hips and shoulders, and learn to use their interrelationship. This will help you get to the ball in a good position for the shot you want to play.

Before going any further I have a couple of questions. Who first decided which foot we should approach the ball with and when? Has the foot position stayed with us since Victorian times when squash was invented?

Traditional foot position

I was always taught that you should approach the ball on the right-hand side of the court with your left foot and on the left-hand side of the court with your right foot. I believe this to be basically correct when we move to the front of the court. After years of trying to get to the ball with the correct foot position, then trying to teach people to do it and failing in all the different areas of the court, I have come to the conclusion that in the heat of a match the priority is, and always has been, getting to the ball as fast as you can, or simply just to get to it! If this is correct, it means that we need to take the most direct route to the ball.

So from here it becomes clear that the next objective should be to have a solid stable base or position when you get to the ball. One that allows you to transfer all the power, or effort, you are putting into your swing through to the ball AND send the ball in the chosen direction.

A solid base is when you have both feet firmly on the floor with your weight evenly spread over them. This permits you to adjust or fine-tune your position at the ball and allows you to transfer your weight from back foot to front foot in the moment of hitting the ball. Note that once your weight is on the front foot you are committed to that position.

Like golf, your feet should be separated so that they are wider than your hips for balance but with the front foot slightly advanced because of the movement towards the ball. Your feet should be pointing in a line perpendicular to the direction we want to hit the ball in, again the same as in golf. This is important because it helps to bring your hips and shoulders into the right position for the shot you want to play.

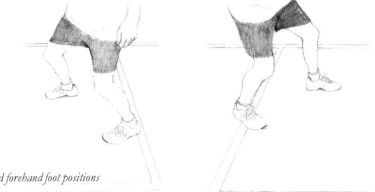

Backhand and forehand foot positions

These are the basic concepts about body position when hitting the ball. Now we will look at the specific shots, keeping in mind what we have just discussed in the previous pages.

Shots

Straight and crosscourt drives

Straight and crosscourt drives are the most common shots used in squash, but perhaps are the least defined. Many players are simply happy if their drive goes in the direction they wanted to hit the ball. All the other shots have clear target areas and objectives which are dictated to us by the situation in the rally that we are battling to win.

Driving the ball well is the result of putting together many components or variables. Firstly, those that are dictated to us by our opponent's shot. Where we are hitting the ball from in the court. Whether the ball is moving fast or slow. Whether the bounce is high or low and if we can get to the ball comfortably. We then add to this our own variables of whether we return the ball by hitting it high or low, hard or fast etc.

Talking recently about this with my mate Dean Lovett*, he came up with an interesting analogy that is worth thinking about.

He said that when a golf player tees off on a par 3 hole, he is aiming to hit the ball directly into a hole that is perhaps 140 metres away. Whereas on a squash court that is 10 metres long, we are normally happy if we just get the ball to go in the general direction we are aiming for. It is clear that a golfer has all the time needed to prepare for the shot, but only has one chance to do it. On a squash court we have very little time to prepare, but we have many more opportunities to hit the target.

What is our target when driving the ball? There are two types of length shots. The first shot is a dying length. Your aim is for the ball to bounce, for the second time, just before it hits the back wall, obliging your opponent to hit the ball before

*Dean was a very good player as a junior and also coached for many years in Brussels and Paris.

it dies in the back corner. The second shot is a full length. The aim is that the ball bounces just before the back wall and obliges your opponent to hit the ball after it has rebounded off the back wall.

Each time you hit the ball you should be choosing one of these drives. Both types of length are an integral part of squash and your game will improve as they become more defined.

I must confess that I personally have given priority to the full length without for one moment taking any importance or value away from the dying length. Here are some of the reasons why.

I define a full length as a ball that bounces less than one metre from the back wall. This definition straight away gives you a clear target to aim at, guaranteeing almost 100% that your opponent will hit the ball after it comes off the wall and that they have moved all the way to the corner to return the ball.

I have seen that it is easy for most players to be conscious of where the ball bounces. Look at the different ways the ball bounces to calculate where your opponent must play their next shot from is a lot more difficult. For example, the heat of the court conditions whether the ball bounces more or less. In warm courts, sometimes, the ball can bounce in the service box and then can be returned after it has come off the back wall. On colder courts the ball must bounce closer to the back wall. Hitting the ball higher or lower on the front wall also conditions the bounce of the ball.

The back corners are unique places, here you have three nicks (side wall with the floor, back wall with the floor and side wall with the back wall) and three different surfaces (floor, back wall and side wall) for the ball to bounce off. Therefore, the chances of getting a 'lucky' bounce or nick are higher there than in any other part of the court. If you reduce your target area to less than half a metre from the back wall you may be surprised as to how 'lucky' you can be. I have often seen that people say sorry when they have a 'lucky' nick or bounce in the back corner. Are they saying, indirectly, that they were not trying to hit the ball to the back corner? I think if they were really sorry they would play a let ;-).

I have noticed that when the ball hits the floor and then a wall in quick succession, it loses speed quicker and the bounce is slightly lower.

When you are aiming for the ball to bounce in the back corner and you miss your target (which we often do) the ball bounces shorter, so further away from the back wall, it then becomes a dying length, which is definitely not a bad shot.

Alternatively if you over hit the ball and it bounces first on the back wall, then on the floor, it means that your opponent is able to return the ball comfortably from a position closer to the middle of the court than you had hoped for. Having said that, I have seen very few players do more than return this ball to the back of the court so we are able to continue playing without having lost any advantage.

When you aim for a dying length and miss your target area the ball bounces shorter, it is then in the middle of the court and this could give the advantage to your opponent because they will be returning the ball from the midcourt area where it is easier for them to play an attacking shot.

The most important reason for focusing your training and play on the full length drive is that as you gain accuracy, your awareness increases and you start to see more clearly the right moment to play the dying length. If you have the habit of hitting a full length it is relatively easy to hit the ball shorter for a dying length. It appears to be more difficult to adjust when you have the habit of playing the dying length and then want to change to hit the ball longer to a full length.

I read once that the Chinese philosopher General Sun Tzu (who wrote the book 'The Art of War') asked his pupils "What is the most important thing we have to prepare for before going into battle?". The replies were along the lines of "we need to be stronger than them", "we need to know our enemy", "we need to fight on grounds that are favourable to us", "we need to be sure that our weapons are better than theirs" etc. Sun Tzu replied that "all the answers could be correct but the most important thing is to ensure that you cannot lose the battle".

This idea, put into a squash context, coincides with Ross Norman's objective which was that he wanted to constantly limit the shot options his opponent had every time they got to the ball. This was to try and avoid giving his opponents any 'free shots', meaning that they were able to hit the ball wherever they wanted.

When I was a teenager I managed to get a copy of Geoff Hunt's book. The main thing I remember from it was his focus on hitting length shots and his comments about the discussions he and his brother would often have about this before going to sleep. All of the great players from the beginning of squash to the present day have been able to define their length game better than their contemporaries. I believe Jahangir Khan's complete dominance was firstly due to better defining, and constantly playing, length. He was, of course, extremely fit but then so were most of his contemporaries.

I have noticed that in match situations when the scores are 9-9 or 10-10 for example, the points are often longer and the ball goes more often to the back corners. Is this because we want to win the point or is it because we don't want to lose the point? Another question I have often asked myself is "why don't we play with this intensity when the score is say 0-0 or 2-2?".

I believe that, where we want to send the ball is an integral part of hitting the ball and should not be considered separately. For this reason I have talked about length shots before going on to describe how you should hit the straight and crosscourt drives.

Having clearly defined in your mind exactly where you want to send the ball before you get to it will definitely help improve your squash.

Drives

Straight and crosscourt drives require the same movement to the ball and racket preparation. It is your body position when you arrive at the ball that changes slightly and dictates the direction of the ball.

We can define three basic areas or situations from where you drive the ball that need slightly different body and foot positions. They are the front of the court, the midcourt area and the back of the court, after the ball has hit the back wall.

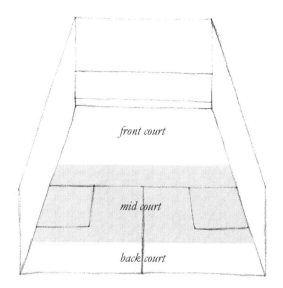

front court

mid court

back court

Now we have to start putting different details together, your movement to the ball and the racket swing, so that you are able to hit the ball from the G Spot in each situation.

Straight drives

The first drive we will look at is hitting the ball straight down the wall from the front of the court. How to move to the front of the court and get to the ball in the correct position was always a bit of a mystery to me. We were given the ideal position with our front foot pointing to the side wall and our back leg and foot behind our body as we stepped forward.

Traditional body position

This has always been pretty much accepted as the best position for hitting the ball. The accepted concept of how we should move to the ball from the T (where we are facing the front wall) has been to draw a line from where the player starts to move forward, from the middle of the court, and then curve around towards the side wall, thus allowing us to be at the ball in this recommended position. I have seen many diagrams showing this line of movement in coaching guides when I was learning how to play and coach. In the last few months I have seen the same concept posted on the internet.

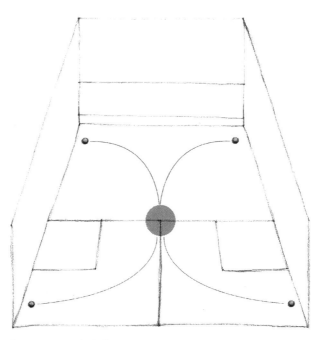

Traditional lines of movement to the ball

I remember trying to move in this curved line to the ball and for years also trying to teach others to do it, as it was accepted as the correct way one should move to the ball. I always found this line of movement unnatural in the controlled situation of a training or coaching session. When it comes to matches this line of movement seems more often than not to disappear because of the need to get to the ball ASAP.

So, looking at the reality of getting to the ball as quickly as possible, I drew a straight line from the T to where we need to hit the ball from. Then I looked at what we need to do to move our bodies from the T and get to the ball with a good solid base from which we are able to hit the ball.

Let's look at our position on the T and how we need to have our body when we are hitting the ball from the G Spot.

Position on the T   *Position at the ball*

You should know what side of the court you will be hitting the ball from as soon as your opponent plays their shot, so in that moment you can start moving and preparing yourself. Some players only start moving when the ball hits the front wall so they will have less time to get to the ball.

You should move forward in a straight line to where you will hit the ball from. In the last step to the ball you need to turn your hips to face the side wall of the court. This automatically brings your shoulders to face the side wall and your front foot is also pointing at the side wall, thus putting yourself in a good position to hit the ball back down the wall.

To this body movement you need to add your racket movement. To be ready to hit the ball the moment you get to it, you need to have your racket prepared when or, even better, before you get to the ball. To achieve this you need to go against one of the most instinctive and natural forms of movement. Whenever you run, your arms move naturally at your sides and normally, the faster you move, the faster your arms move. So you need to change this instinctive habit so that your racket is prepared when you get to the ball.

When your opponent hits the ball you know what side of the court the ball is going to. This is the moment in which you can start preparing the racket. At the same time you start moving towards the ball you should be moving your racket back. In this way you will almost always be ready to hit the ball as soon as you get to it.

Although your body and feet position are the same when you get to the ball on both the forehand and backhand sides of the court, you need to note that the G Spot is in a different position in relation to your body. There is a certain amount of logic in this affirmation, as on the backhand your racket arm is in front of your body when you get to the ball and on the forehand it is on the back side of your body.

front shoulder   *back shoulder*

On the backhand side the G Spot is in line with your racket arm or front shoulder and the side wall when you get to the ball.

On the forehand side the G Spot is again in a line between the shoulder of your racket arm and the side wall. On this side of the court it is your back shoulder. This means that on the forehand the ball should almost (but not quite) be behind your body when you hit it. So to have the ball in this position, when you get to the ball, your last step should place your leading foot slightly in front of the ball so that it is in line with your racket shoulder when you hit it. On the forehand it is therefore even more important that you move your body forward to the ball and resist the temptation of waiting for the ball to come to the G Spot.

When you put together this movement to the ball with the racket preparation and then hit the ball from the G Spot, the ball will always go straight down the side wall. I would add at this stage that putting these details all together is often easier said than done because of the speed of squash. First it requires you to become conscious of the different movements required and then start to develop the habit of moving in this way.

Note that in a normal game situation when you have got to the ball and have hit it down the wall, you would have been in the right position and instinctively hit the ball from the G Spot. With training and more detailed awareness of your movement, you can develop consistency and increase your precision in what is not only one of the most basic shots in squash but also one of the most important. In the chapter about training we will talk more about how to work on and develop these habits.

Crosscourt drives from the front

Your movement to the ball and racket swing are the same for the crosscourt drives. All you need to do is adjust your body position when you are hitting the ball. It is the line of your shoulders that, combined with hitting the ball from the G Spot, gives direction to the ball. So for the crosscourt, your shoulders and hips are facing the front corner of the court and your feet are pointing to the same front corner.

Forehand cross court position　　　　　　　　　　　　*Backhand cross court position*

Ideally when hitting the ball you should have the minimum amount of shoulder movement. There is sometimes a tendency with crosscourt drives to move your shoulders as you are hitting the ball. Part of the reason for this movement is that you are following or watching the ball after you have hit it. Another possible reason is that sometimes you have the ball in front of the G Spot which obliges you to turn your shoulders so that you can hit the ball cleanly.

Again you need to have a clear target area. I personally prefer aiming for the side wall or nick about a metre from the back wall. This way you are ensuring that your opponents have had to move the maximum distance possible to return the ball. Some say that the line of this ball passes too close to your opponent on the T. Others prefer aiming for the back of the service box. This line ensures that your opponent cannot volley the ball but is able to return it with just one or two steps from the T. You can, of course, look at other target areas.

I think you should first try the various possible lines for your crosscourt shot and then choose the option that is best suited to your game. This definition with a clear cross target area will help you to create a habit. Having this habit of hitting the ball to a specific area will allow you then to choose or vary the crosscourt shot according to where your opponent is.

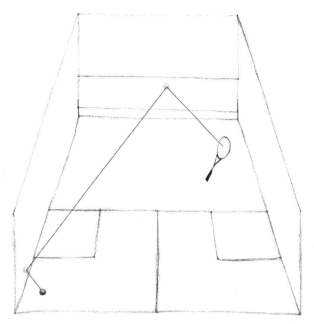

Cross court shot line

Straight drive from midcourt

The midcourt area is from the centre line to just behind the service box. This second area requires a slightly different way of moving to the ball, which in turn conditions your body position when you get to the ball.

In this area you generally have little time to get to a ball, as it is often moving fast and you are obliged to move quickly, and must hit it immediately.

Starting from the T, where you are facing the front wall, the first movement is a couple of side steps towards the side wall and the ball. Then the last step to the ball is with the leg that is closest to the ball (the right leg on the right side of the court and the left leg on the left side of the court). In this last step you again need to turn your hips and shoulders to face, or be parallel with, the side wall. As the distance to the ball varies slightly with each shot you play in this area you may have to add a step or two in the sequence. The priority is to take the shortest route to the ball and finish with your hips and shoulders parallel with the side wall.

You then need to add your racket movement to this process. In the moment you start moving towards the ball you can start to prepare your racket so that it is back and you can hit the ball as soon as you get to it. Given the little time you have to hit the ball in this area of the court, having your racket back and prepared before you get to the ball will increase your shot options.

Mid court forehand position   *Mid Court backhand position*

Crosscourt drives from the midcourt area

A crosscourt shot is often the easiest option in this area because of the way you move to the ball. You are almost naturally in a position for a crosscourt shot. The movement to the ball is the same as for the straight drive, with one or two side steps and then you turn your hips and shoulders so that you are ready to hit the ball as soon as you get to it. Here your shoulders should be pointing towards the middle of the front wall, which is the direction you want to hit the ball.

The target you should aim for depends a little on the speed of your opponent's shot. What is clear is that you should always ensure that your shot obliges your opponent to return the ball from a position further back in the court than the position from where you are playing your shot. If the ball is moving very fast and you have very little time it is probably better to take a little speed off the ball, hit it higher on the wall and be sure that the ball hits the back wall thus giving yourself time to recover to the T. If you have more time to hit the ball you can look to hit it hard, to a dying length, to put pressure on your opponent.

Driving from the back of the court

Your body position to hit the ball after it has bounced off the back wall is different from the two areas we have already talked about.

You often have a little more time to hit the ball from the back corners because you wait for the ball to rebound off the back wall. Here your body position is a little more upright and can be likened to that of a golf player. For the straight drive your shoulders and hips are parallel to the side wall and your feet are also pointing at the side wall. Your feet are separated and your legs are slightly bent at the knees with your weight evenly placed over both legs. This position allows you to adjust both feet when the ball bounces off the back wall so that you can hit the ball from the G Spot. This position also allows us to react instantly if the ball bounces unexpectedly, as it sometimes does in the back corners.

Back court forehand position   *Back court backhand position*

For the crosscourt drive from the back of the court your shoulders should be pointing towards the middle of the front wall or in the direction you want to hit the ball. Your hip and feet position also need to be adjusted accordingly.

Although we have more time here, you should start preparing your racket as you are moving to the ball, like you have done when hitting the ball from the front or midcourt areas. This extra time should then be used to ensure that you hit the ball as well and as precisely as you can. From the back of the court you should be aiming to play the full length or the dying length. It is important to define and play both options.

Serve

To serve, at least one foot must be in the service box and is not allowed to touch the line. If it touches the line, or is out of the box, it is a fault and the player loses the serve and the point. There are various ways to serve but the main objective should be to get the ball into the opposite back corner and to ensure that your opponent is not able to hit the ball easily. The best way to do this is to make sure that the ball touches the side wall before your opponent can hit it.

On the forehand side, face the front wall, place one foot in the service box and one out with your toes of both feet pointing to the front wall and have your racket stationary in the start position. Throw the ball up gently 45o towards the side wall and hit it high to the middle of the front wall, with the objective of hitting the side wall high, just behind the opponent's service box so that it drops into that back corner.

Forehand serve

On the backhand side, face the opposite side wall with both feet in the service box. Your racket is in the starting position and stationary. Take one step forward with leg closest to the front wall and throw the ball gently towards the G Spot in front of your racket arm. Hit it again high to the middle of the front wall with the objective of hitting the side wall high, just behind the service box on the opposite side of the court so that it drops into that back corner.

Backhand serve

The serve in squash does not have the same importance or instant impact on the game as does the serve, for example, in tennis. It is relatively simple to play but a bad serve that gives your opponent an easy return can be decisive. Given this, it is good to train yourself mentally to be aware of how good each of your own serves are as soon as you have hit them. In the moment you see that your serve is not good and your opponent may have a 'free shot' you should look immediately to see if they are preparing to attack it or even kill the ball with, for example, a nick shot. If this is the case you have a better chance returning their attacking shot because you saw at the earliest moment where they wanted to hit the ball to and you are able to move in that direction immediately to try and return it. If you see they are not going to attack your bad serve you should be relieved and take note to make the next serve better.

As soon as you have hit the serve you should move to the middle of the court, or the T, so that you are in the best position for your next shot.

Return of serve

To return a serve you should stand about one racket length, in diagonal, from the back corner of the service box. Better players will stand further forward to pressure their opponent's serve.

Forehand and backhand return of serve positions

Your first objective is to volley the ball. Your next objective is to volley it before it touches the side wall. If this is not possible, volley it after it comes off the side wall. Finally if you are not able to volley it, you have to hit it after it comes off the back wall. In each case we should be trying to return the serve to a back corner so you can move comfortably to the T, thus neutralising the server's advantaged position.

A good serve can create indecision in the person returning it, especially when the ball is close to the wall at the moment they would like to hit it. The doubts that come to mind are "should I volley it or let it bounce?", "do I hit it before or after it hits the side wall?", "should I let it hit the back wall or not?". A simple rule for these kind of doubts is that you should always hit the ball at the first opportunity you have and not wait, hoping the next opportunity may be easier. This is a good rule for any situation in the court where you are doubting whether to hit the ball before or after it touches the wall. I made this rule for myself after feeling silly quite a few times, having decided to hit the ball after it had touched the wall only to find that it died on the wall and I was unable to return it. It also means that you have to hit the ball earlier, thus applying more pressure on your opponent.

I have seen that volleying the return of a serve after it has hit the side wall can create a moment of insecurity in the receiver. This is because when the ball hits the side wall it changes direction and speed and drops in a more vertical line giving us very little time to play it. Thus making it one of the more difficult situations in which we have to volley the ball. Normally you move your racket horizontally towards the ball, but in this case you are cutting the line of the ball which is falling vertically, so your timing must be near perfect to hit the ball well. I have noticed that in the moment you choose to hit the ball, if you have your racket back and stationary, and move the racket in a semi-vertical line up towards the falling ball, it is consistently easier and more comfortable to hit.

Given that there are no second serves in squash, I think the receiver should keep an eye on whether or not their opponent's foot remains in the box when they serve. Apart from the point that can be won or lost, it should be part of developing global consciousness of what is going on in the court.

Boast

The boast is the shot that hits the side wall before hitting the front wall. It is used both as a defensive shot, when you are unable to return the ball directly to the front wall because it has gone behind you, or an attacking shot, when you want to move your opponent to the front of the court. In both cases it can end up being a winning shot.

There are two types of boast, the three wall boast that after hitting the ball to the side wall and front wall it then hits low, or ideally in the nick, on the other side wall. The two wall boast is one that bounces on the floor after hitting the front wall and bounces for the second time just before the ball hits the third wall.

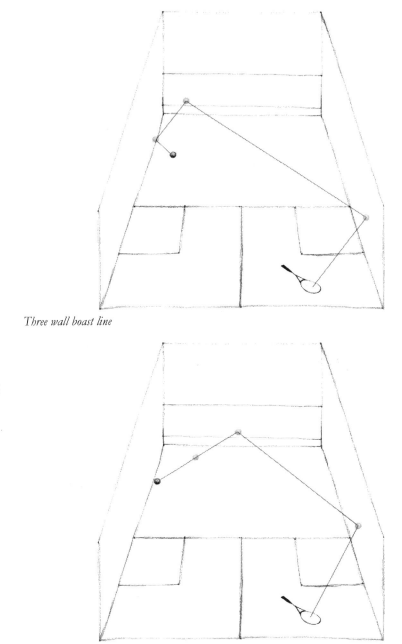

Three wall boast line

Two wall boast line

Over the years I have sometimes heard people defending one or the other options as the boast shot that should be used, suggesting there are sometimes two schools of thought. I believe both options should be an integral part of your game and the challenge is to choose the right moment to play each one. I have seen that different people instinctively prefer one over the other and therefore develop that one and thus argue it is the best option. In the end both types of boast have been used effectively forever which indicates that both options are valid options in the right moment.

The racket movement when hitting the boast is the same as, for example, a straight drive. It is important that you hit behind and slightly below the centre of the ball or underneath the ball. Ensuring the ball leaves your racket in a slightly upward direction will help it to get to the front wall. If the ball leaves your racket horizontally to the side wall it will lose height as soon as it hits the side wall, reducing the chances of it getting to the front wall. I have seen that if you have your racket face slightly more open than normal, the boast becomes more consistent, and stays lower when it hits the side wall. Note that you should not confuse having the racket face open with cutting the ball which would be a recipe for disaster. I can't explain yet exactly why this helps with the boast but have seen for myself and with people I have coached that it does help. You have to experiment a little yourself to find the right solution for you.

Each time you play a boast you should define very clearly which boast you wish to play. I personally prefer to start with the three wall boast because the body position required is more difficult and at the limit of the body's range of positions that are used for a boast. If you have a clear idea in your head, and are able to create the basic habit of hitting this boast, in the moment you have the opportunity to play the two wall boast it is easier to adjust your body position to play it. If it is the other way round where you have the habit of the two wall boast and want to play the three wall boast, it is more difficult to find the right position for that boast.

I was told when I was young that you should imagine that the side wall is glass and that you can see the court next door. Aim to hit the ball toward the opposite front corner of the court next door to have the correct angle so that the ball hits the three walls and hopefully the nick.

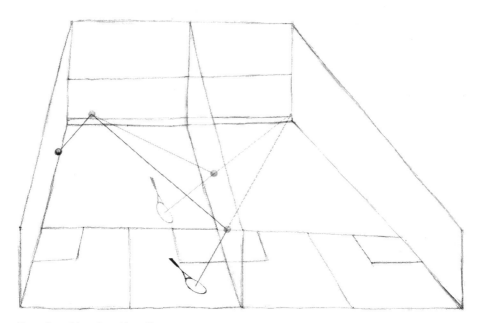

Boast line with a glass side wall

Try this. Start in the back corner and aim your shoulders at the far front corner of the court next door (in some cases this will need to be an imaginary court) and hit the ball. Do the same from the back of the service box, from the front of the service box and finally from halfway between the service box to the front wall. If your shoulders are aimed correctly at the far corner of the court next door, in each case the ball should hit the three walls and return along the floor to you (make sure you hit it high enough).

For the three wall boast you need to be facing the back corner so that your shoulders are pointing to the side wall. You need to have your racket back, prepared and stationary and your feet should be separated with your weight evenly placed.

Boast body position

This position allows you to move or adjust your body quickly to where you need to hit the ball from. It allows you to react instantly if the ball does not bounce the way you expect it to, as it does occasionally in the back corners. If you get to the ball with a little bit of time to prepare yourself, your foot movement in the back corners can be likened to that of a boxer, karate or Kung Fu fighter where you move both feet simultaneously, allowing you to move your body in a balanced way to the best position for the boast. This movement also allows you to fine-tune your body position so that you are able to hit the ball from the G Spot. It is important that you try and have a minimum of shoulder movement in the moment you hit the ball. This will give you more consistency and help to reduce unforced errors.

If you are under a lot of pressure the priority is to get to the ball as soon as possible, so any foot position that allows you to do this is good. In this kind of situation you need to try and have your shoulders aiming in the direction you want to hit the ball and have your racket back before you arrive at the ball so that you can hit it immediately.

When you have all your weight on one foot (normally the front foot) it is much more difficult to react and recover the unexpected bounces of the ball in the back corners. This is also why it is important that the racket is back as early as possible so that you can react in a split second if necessary.

If the ball has gone past you and you have no alternative but to play a boast either because you are getting to the ball with very little time or simply because the ball is very low in the corner and again you have very little time to hit it, having your racket back and prepared is even more important.

The three wall boast is the more defensive option of the two types of boasts. The fact that your opponent is not able to hit the ball until it has hit the three walls can give you a little more time to recover your position. Also if your boast hits low on the third side wall, it can limit the shot options of your opponent.

The two wall boast is equally used as a defensive shot. It is the better option of the two types of boast to play as an attacking shot. This boast is played from positions in the back corners of the court and all the way up to the front of the court.

When in the back of the court your shoulders should aim roughly towards where the half court line meets the side wall (it varies slightly depending on your own position) or have a body position half way between the three wall boast and the straight drive. You are aiming for the ball to bounce, for the second time, before it hits the third wall, forcing your opponent to get to the ball and play quickly. You oblige them to move faster and test their ability to return the ball under pressure. It is important to remember that if they are getting to and hitting the ball earlier, you too will have less time to recover from your shot. In this situation it is important that you are able to recover to the centre of the court before your opponent hits the ball or you will be giving the advantage to your opponent.

After having looked at the two types of boast I would say that your objective should be to clearly choose one of the two types of boast, depending on the situation, and not simply play a boast without definition.

Reverse angle boast

If you are on the forehand side of the court, for example, this boast hits the side wall on the backhand side of the court before hitting the front wall and then finishes close to the side wall on the forehand side of the court. You hit the ball hard so the ball moves very fast to the front of the court. This shot is commonly used by lower levelled players when they need to hit the ball to the front of the court and are not confident enough to try a drop shot. I learnt to play it from a young age and I found it to be a very useful shot at every level of squash that I played. When the ball comes back to you very quickly to the middle of the court, and your opponent is out of position behind you, and you do not have time to prepare yourself for a drop shot, the reverse angle boast is a relatively low risk way of getting the ball to the front corner. It forces your opponent to move very fast to that part of the court. It can also be an effective way to finish a point. At higher levels it is a useful way to test your opponent, you will see if they are paying attention to how and where you are hitting the ball as it is a shot they may not have expected you to play.

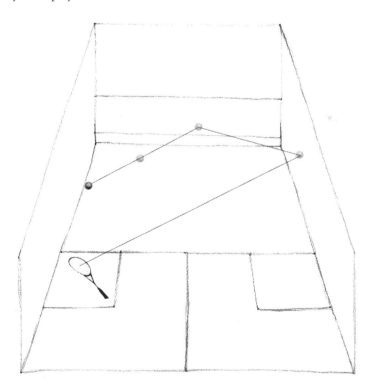

Reverse angle boast line

To play the reverse angle boast effectively you must hit the ball well in front of your body, so that you let the ball go past the G Spot position of the crosscourt drive. Doing this, you can deceive your opponent because your body position is similar to that of a straight or crosscourt drive.

Skid boast

You play the skid boast from the back half of the court. You hit the ball high on the side wall so that after it hits the front wall it lands in the opposite back corner. It can be useful when you need to move your opponent to the other side of the court and are not able to get into a position to play a crosscourt shot.

You hit the ball high on the wall so that it 'skids' to the front wall and then lands in the opposite back corner.

Be careful with this shot because if the ball hits the side wall at the wrong angle it slows down quickly and you can give an easy volley to your opponent. It is important to experiment with this shot before you use it in a match situation.

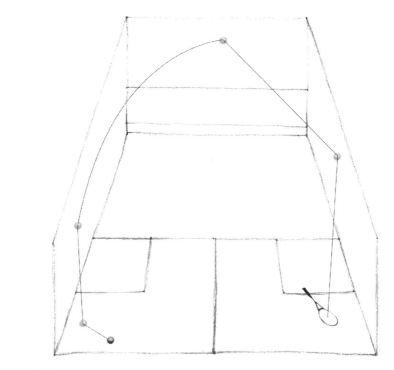

Skid boast line

Drop shot

The drop shot is probably the most common of the high precision shots in squash. It is also where an awareness of hitting the ball from the G Spot can be the most helpful. For most of the other shots played in squash it goes unnoticed if the ball hits on the wall, for example, 10 to 20 (or more) centimetres higher or lower than the area you were aiming for. With the drop shot you immediately see if the ball has gone to the area you were aiming for.

The first thing to have very clear is that you need to move your body to the ball so that you are at the G Spot when you are going to hit it, and not waiting for the ball to come to you. If the ball comes to you in a good position for the drop shot, as it sometimes does, it should be taken as a bonus or, you could even say, as a present :-) . Being able to play your drop shots well should not depend on if the ball has come to you in a good position, but on how you have positioned yourself.

The drop shot is mostly played from the midcourt and front court areas.

When your opponent has played a weaker shot from the back or midcourt areas and the ball has returned to the midcourt area, this is the moment you can play your drop shot. If your opponent has played a weak shot from the front of the court you should almost always play the dying length shot. I have often seen that players play their drop shots in this situation just because they see an opportunity to play a drop shot to perhaps win the point. They are not conscious of the fact that their opponent is not far away from the ball, so has a good chance of returning the ball unless they play an excellent drop shot.

As soon as you see the opportunity to play your drop shot you should start moving towards the ball. You have to turn your body to face the side wall with your shoulders pointing in the direction of the front corner. Your feet are pointing at the side wall, your body slightly crouched. That is, your legs are bent with your weight over both feet and your upper body leaning forward. Your racket should already have been back and prepared as soon as you saw what side of the court you were going to play the ball from.

Your racket movement is the same as when you drive the ball, simply with less speed. It is very important that as the racket moves down behind the ball and that you maintain the natural forearm movement, where the racket head falls behind your wrist as it moves towards the ball. As the wrist comes in line with the G Spot is the moment when the racket face catches up and impacts with the ball. The face of the racket should be slightly open. From here the racket should be briefly moving in the direction you want the ball to go, and then should finish naturally in a vertical position close to your body on the backhand and in the line of your shoulders on the forehand.

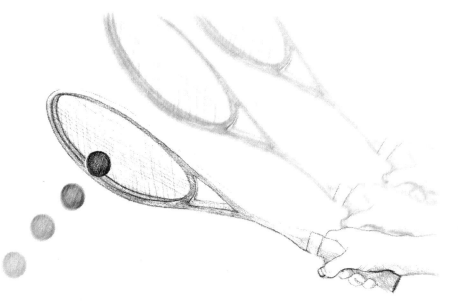

Racket movement through the ball

For the drop shot the racket face should be more open than with the other shots. You should experiment by opening the face of the racket more or less to find the right position for you and to better understand the effect it has on the ball. This helps to take the speed off the ball as it comes to you and gives it a very slight spinning effect so that it drops a little when it hits the front wall.

This spinning effect from the open-faced racket often leads people to believe that the ball is being 'cut'. If your drop shot is based on a racket movement that 'cuts' the ball you will have less consistency and a higher error rate.

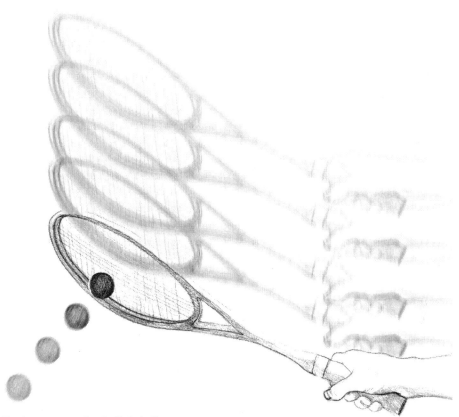

Racket movement "cutting" the ball

Pay special attention to ensure that your forearm movement is moving your racket from behind and through to the ball. This will ensure that the ball goes to the front wall in the direction you are aiming.

Your target area is about 10 centimetres above the tin so that you have a margin for error and the ball stays close to the side wall. This will limit your opponent's shot options when they return the ball.

Many coaches say that the ball should bounce on the floor close to the side wall after it has hit the front wall. I have noticed that if the ball touches the side wall soon after hitting the front wall it slows down quicker and the bounce is lower. It is good to be aware of both options and experiment with them to find out what is right for your own drop shot. With this idea, where you play the drop shot from can also be a determining factor, so it is important that you take this into account as well. For example, if you are playing your drop shot from somewhere close to the side wall, it is easier to have the ball bounce on the floor so that it stays close to the side wall. If you are further towards the middle of the court you can use the side wall to slow the ball down.

Now to play your drop shot you need to put together all of the different details that we have discussed.

On the backhand side, you move forward to the ball watching it closely. When you get to the position from where you will hit the ball, stop with a balanced body position and your racket prepared. At this moment you need to have clearly in your mind that your objective is to hit the ball from the G Spot. With this focus, when the ball is arriving at the G Spot (which is in front of your racket arm shoulder) you hit the ball in a straight line to the target area in the front corner.

Backhand drop shot position

The forehand drop shot is a little more complicated because the ball is almost (but not quite) behind your body when you should hit it. This means that you have to move forward more to get your body in a position where the G Spot is in the line between the shoulder of your racket arm and the side wall (which on the forehand is your back shoulder). To have the ball in this position when you get to it, your last step should place your leading foot slightly in front of the ball. Having got to the ball with your racket prepared and watching it closely, you focus on hitting it when it gets to the G Spot.

On the forehand it is important to resist the temptation of waiting for the ball to come back to the G Spot and not moving your body forward.

Forehand drop shot

For both backhand and forehand drop shots it is important that your shoulders are aimed in the direction you want to hit the ball and that they remain as stationary as possible while you are playing the shot.

Drop shot from the front of the court

When your opponent has played a boast or drop shot to the front of the court, and you want to reply to their shot with a drop shot of your own, the target area is the same as the drop shot from the midcourt area. As the ball is often lower you have to move further forward in the court to get to the ball, giving you less time to prepare your body position. Playing a drop shot from here can be a little more complicated. It is good to remember that, in this situation, you are often just one or two metres away from the front wall, so in the closest possible position from your target area. This in itself should mean that you have more chance of hitting your target. Yet in reality it is not an easy shot, as you have very little time to hit the ball.

As the ball is low, your body position should also be as low as possible. Your shoulders should be aimed at the target area, your feet pointing towards the side wall and your racket back and prepared. This allows you to move your racket from behind and through to the ball, gently guiding it to your target area. Here your racket preparation is vital and will allow you to hit the ball well, even if you have not been able to get to the ball with correct body position.

Crosscourt drop shots

The target area for the crosscourt drop shot is clearly the nick or low on the side wall so that the ball dies quickly (that is, it bounces twice before your opponent can return it). Here the golf analogy of aiming for a hole-in-one that I talked about earlier in the book is even more valid. When you are looking for this kind of precision you must be as precise as possible with all different details that make up a drop shot.

This need for precision dictates that when you have got to the ball (in the same way that I have explained for the straight drop shot) that, on the forehand side your shoulders and hips are aiming at the front backhand corner and, on the backhand side, your shoulders and hips are aiming at the front forehand corner. Your racket must be back and prepared, your weight evenly balanced over both feet (as in golf). You must be watching the ball closely so that, as soon as it arrives at the G Spot, you are able to hit it. Remember your racket should move from behind and through the ball and it is important that the racket face is open.

Pay special attention to not move your shoulders when you are hitting the ball. Also that you do not start moving back to the T before you have completely finished playing your shot. These are common mistakes when playing drop shots that, in the end, reduce your ability to be precise and consistent.

I think one of the most common reasons people hit their drop shots down, or into the tin, is because they are thinking about the chance they have to win the point. This can create a certain amount of nerves or doubts in the player with thoughts like "should I try to win this point or not?", "this is the chance I have been waiting for" etc. These kinds of thoughts then pushes the player, consciously or subconsciously, to hit the ball as close as they can to the top of the tin, therefore noticeably increasing the amount of risk. The other thought that causes problems is "I hope I don't make a mistake". In reality this fear of making a mistake or the excessive desire to win the point distracts the player from all the practical details required to play the drop shot successfully.

If you are focused purely on the details of the drop shot such as your body position, your racket preparation, where you want to hit the ball etc., the level of nerves or doubts can be noticeably reduced. Being focused on hitting the ball 10 to 20 centimetres above the tin or simply hitting it 'up' reduces the number of balls that hit the tin. There are very few players who are able to hit their target constantly, so by consciously aiming for 10 to 20 centimetres above the tin you will have a margin for error. I personally missed the target regularly and when the ball hit lower than I had planned for, it often ended up being a great drop shot.

Two more possible reasons as to why you may have hit your drop shot into the tin are firstly, that you have hit the ball before it is at or in front of the G Spot. Secondly, you have not had the racket back so the racket must move in a downward direction when you are hitting the ball. If you can see why your drop shot has hit the tin, you can work on correcting it when you play the next one.

Volleys

Volleying the ball in squash is very important. Given that the squash court is only six metres wide you constantly have opportunities to volley the ball. Firstly you use it to put pressure on your opponent. The more you volley, the less time your opponent has to return the ball and are forced to move faster to the ball. Secondly, you can also use it to finish or win points with attacking shots to the front of the court.

As opposed to tennis where volleying the ball is mainly used as an attacking shot, the volley in squash is extremely varied and is used as an attacking or a defensive shot. There are overhead volleys, like in tennis, and then you have volley drives, volley boasts, volley drop shots and volley lobs.

Due to the high speed at which squash is played you often have very little time to volley the ball, so your racket preparation is again very important if you want consistency and accuracy. As we talked about earlier, the ball bouncing is the subconscious signal for many people to start moving their rackets to hit the ball. Obviously with the volley you don't have this clear reference point. I think this leads to some players not seeing the opportunity to volley until it is too late, thus they have to let the ball go to the back wall and play it from there. The fact that you can often play the ball after it hits the back wall encourages some people to let it go past and hit it after it has bounced off the back wall.

You should be constantly looking for the opportunity to volley the ball.

When volleying you need to pay special attention to your body position. You need a stable balanced position from the moment you start hitting the ball until you have finished playing the volley. An unstable body position is a common cause for mistakes when volleying.

When moving the racket above your head your centre of balance is higher than with any other shot, so it is easier to lose your balance especially given the speed at which you move around the squash court. Being aware of this helps you to look for the stable and solid position which is such an important part of overhead volleying.

Another common problem is that players start moving away from the ball or back to the T before they have finished hitting the volley. This is, in part, because they are worried that the ball may come back too close to their bodies. This fear then makes the player move away even faster after they have hit the ball, which in turn increases the chances that the ball comes back close to their bodies, thus creating a catch 22 situation.

You should only move away from where you are hitting the ball once you have completed your racket movement and finished the follow through. You do not have to move until you have finished your shot, so do not worry that you may be in your opponent's way to the ball. After you have completely finished your shot move back to the T and give your opponent clear access to the ball. Your priority is playing your volley well.

A good test to see if you are in the correct position when volleying is to check that you have your feet in the same position from when you start until you finish playing your volley. If you manage to do this, it normally means that you have had a good body position for your shot.

Overhead forehand volley

We will start discussing the overhead volley as this is the most obvious or known form of volleying. You play the overhead volley when your opponent has hit the ball high and with less speed towards the back of the court.

Your position is more upright than for the other shots and your feet are separated. Your knees are very slightly bent for balance. Your shoulders are pointing in the direction you want to hit the ball. Your hips are in line with your shoulders and your feet are pointing towards the side wall.

You have three possible target areas. To the front corner, when your opponent has played their shot from the back or midcourt area. A dying length, where the ball bounces for the second time just before it gets to the back wall. A full length, with the ball bouncing in the back corner so your opponent must hit the ball after it has bounced off the back wall. Note that all these target areas ensure that your opponent will not be returning your shot from the middle of the court.

Volleying the ball higher or lower on the front wall depends on where the ball is and when you hit it. To hit it lower on the front wall you must hit the ball when it is slightly in front of the shoulder of your racket arm. To hit the ball straight to the front wall, the ball is in line with your shoulder. To hit the ball higher on the front wall, it needs to be hit from slightly behind your shoulder.

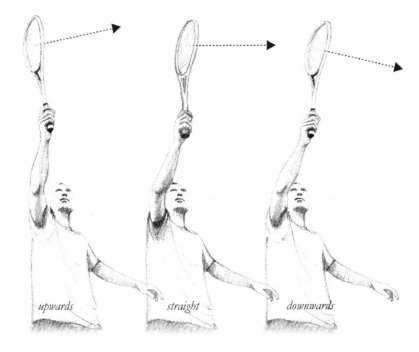

upwards   *straight*   *downwards*

The volley G Spot to hit the ball

The moment to start preparing the racket again is when your opponent has played their shot and you see which side of the court they have hit the ball to. As their shot moves toward the front wall you should start to see if you are going to have the opportunity to volley the ball, so this is when you should start to prepare your racket.

To prepare your racket for the overhead volley on the forehand, it should be stationary behind your body with the upper arm in the same line as your shoulders, your elbow should be bent and the racket behind your head.

Racket prepared   *Forehand volley G Spot*   *Forehand volley follow through*

From here as you move your racket forward towards the ball, your forearm and racket fall behind your head. They catch up with your elbow and upper arm when they are arrive at the G Spot, which is again perpendicular to the shoulder of your racket arm. For the overhead volley it is at a full arm's length above your head. The follow through after hitting the ball will then take your racket down to the level of your hips, then it should continue upwards and finish by your other shoulder in a natural, fluid movement. This ensures that your racket will guide the ball in the chosen direction. It is important that your racket does not finish down by your hips as you will lose consistency.

The face of your racket should be open for most volleys. Again, you can experiment by varying the open face of your racket to find the position that is best for you and the shot that you are playing. It is good to develop your awareness of these slight adjustments and how they can help the ball move to the front wall more consistently.

Overhead backhand volley

The overhead volley on the backhand is where there is the most noticeable difference between forehand and backhand shots. On the backhand, we do not have the same power if we hit the ball high above our heads. If you hit the ball at the same height as you do on the forehand, you can only guide the ball in the direction you want to send it. To hit the backhand volley with the same power as you do on the forehand you need to hit it when it is lower, so at head height.

To prepare your racket for the overhead volley on the backhand your racket hand is stationary, above your left shoulder for right-handers and above your right shoulder for left-handers. Your racket is almost falling down behind your back.

Backhand volley follow through   *Backhand volley G Spot*   *Racket prepared*

From here your racket starts moving forward towards the G Spot. Your racket falls to a horizontal position above your shoulder and then catches up with your upper arm and elbow at the G Spot when your arm is perpendicular to your racket shoulder.

Your follow through continues and finishes with your upper arm in line with your shoulders and your forearm in a vertical position. Your racket should not go as low as it does on the forehand (to hip level) as you don't have the same strength high in the air on the backhand side.

Overhead volley kill

People tend to mainly associate the overhead volley with the opportunity to kill the ball or to hit it low and hard. You shouldn't automatically hit the overhead volley to the front of the court. You need to take into account other factors. Firstly you should be aware of where your opponent is, then from where you would like them to return the next ball. Being aware of your own body position should also be a defining factor in deciding where you will hit the ball. If you have not been able to get into a good, balanced position you shouldn't hit the ball low to the front of the court.

Precision shots need precision, not just with the racket but also with all of the details that make up a shot. The more of these details that you are able to put together consciously, the more you will reduce the risk of making a mistake, which is always present when playing the ball to the front of the court. You will also become more consistent with your shots. Building this awareness takes time, you cannot start doing it just because you have read or thought about it, you need to work at it over time.

Another common error when wanting to hit your volley low on the front wall is that people think they need to hit on top of the ball to bring it down. This seems to increase the probability of 'dragging' the ball down into the tin or even worse. To avoid this, try thinking about aiming to hit the ball in a straight line to your target area. It helps to reduce the risk of 'dragging' the ball down.

Remember you should always be hitting the ball with an open-faced racket. This will help you to hit the ball in a straight line to the front wall. I again recommend that you should experiment with opening your racket face more and less. These slight adjustments are often surprising and will give you more options at the time of hitting the ball.

It is good to understand the reasons why your volley kill shot may not have gone as planned. It can help you avoid repeating the same mistakes regularly.

Straight volley kill shots

Once you have your body position and racket prepared with your shoulders aimed at the front corner you can hit the ball firmly, but not hard, so that the ball stays in the front corner. If you hit the ball hard there is more of a chance that the ball will return to the midcourt area where your opponent has more opportunity to return the ball.

Aim to hit the ball about 10 centimetres above the tin and then, if possible, have the ball hit the side wall. Hitting the side wall here slows the ball and the ball bounces less.

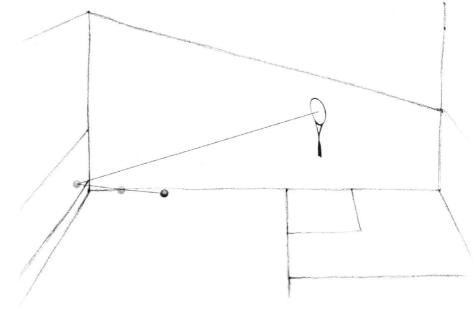

Straight volley kill shot line

Crosscourt volley nick shots

This is probably the squash dream shot. The shot that every player loves to play or at least would like to play better and more often. The target is to hit the nick (the angle where the side wall meets the floor) about one to two metres from the front wall so the ball does not bounce, or at least bounces very little.

Given the precision required you need to be precise with your body position, racket preparation and movement (as described earlier). You aim your shoulders across the court at the front corner. You hit the ball firmly, with a slightly open racket face, to the front wall, about one metre from the front corner, and then have the ball bounce in the nick or low on the side wall so it bounces very little. As you become more confident or practiced, you can hit the ball harder. The follow through is important, having the racket finish up by your other shoulder on the forehand, or in line with your shoulders and at shoulder level, will help you to be more consistent with this shot.

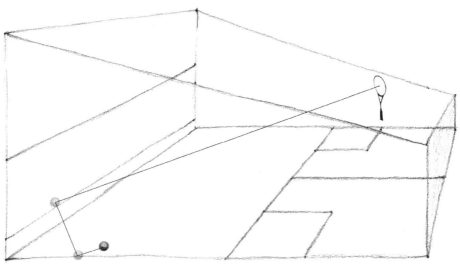

Crosscourt volley nick shot line

Overhead dying length volley

This is the volley that can be most likened to a tennis volley smash because you are hitting the ball hard with full arm movement and a flat racket face. The objective is that the second bounce of the ball is in the back corner, forcing your opponent to hit the ball from behind the service box and before it bounces for the second time. It is better to play this volley straight down the wall, aiming for the ball to stay very close to the wall.

A crosscourt dying length is not as effective as the straight volley because the ball tends to bounce off the side wall giving your opponent more room to hit it.

It is most commonly played when your opponent has played a lob either from the front or back of the court. It is difficult to win the point with this volley, but it can often force a weaker shot which will allow you to finish the point with your next shot.

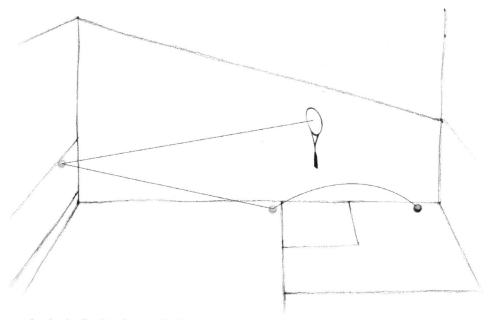

Overhead volley dying length volley line

Your body position and racket preparation are the same as the other overhead volleys.

The target area on the front wall varies, depending on the height of the ball when you are hitting it, how hard you hit it and where in the court you are hitting it from. I believe it is better to focus on having the ball close to the wall and bouncing for the second time just before it hits the back wall. You should experiment with different target areas to find the best option for your game.

Volley drop shot

You normally play the volley drop shot from the midcourt area when the ball is between hip and head height. When you volley the ball in this area, the ball is often coming to you quickly so you have little time to hit it. For this reason the racket movement is slightly shorter than that of a normal drop shot. Your racket needs to be prepared with an open racket face as soon as you see what side of the court it has been hit to.

On the backhand your racket hand should be prepared at chest level and not up by your shoulder, as is the case with the drop shot. From here you move the racket in a straight line to the ball, hitting it gently, but firmly, to the same target area on the front wall as the drop shot, 10 centimetres above the tin and close to the side wall. The follow through is shorter because it is a natural continuation of this reduced racket movement. It is important that the racket finishes in a vertical position.

On the forehand your racket hand is again prepared at chest level, behind your body and in line with your shoulders. You move your racket in a straight line to the ball, hitting gently but firmly to the same target area on the front wall, 10 centimetres above the tin and close to the side wall. Your racket finishes naturally in a vertical position close to your body.

Your movement to the ball is the same as described when driving the ball from the midcourt area. You are at the T, where you are facing the front wall, the first movement is a couple of side steps towards the side wall and the ball. Then the last step to the ball is with the leg that is closest to the ball. The right leg on the right side of the court and the left leg on the left side of the court. In this last step you should turn your hips and shoulders to face or be parallel with the side wall. The distance to the ball varies slightly with each shot you play in this area so you may have to add a step or two in the sequence. The priority is to take the shortest route to the ball and finish with your hips and shoulders parallel with the side wall.

Playing the volley drop shot straight to the front corner is generally more effective than playing it crosscourt. By this I mean that your forehand volley drop shot should be played to the front forehand corner and your backhand volley drop shot to the front backhand corner.

This is more effective because your opponent will have to move to the T and then change direction to return the ball. When you play it crosscourt your opponent has direct and easy access to the ball. They can also see where it is going as soon as you have hit it. When you play the crosscourt drop shot it is important that it hits the side wall or nick after hitting the front wall.

Forehand volley drop shot position   *Backhand volley drop shot position*

Lob

The lob is a defensive shot that you normally use from the front of the court when you are struggling to get to the ball. Slowing the ball down and hitting it high will give you time to recover your court position. It can also be used as a tactical variation in your game to upset the rhythm of your opponent.

The lob is the only squash shot where we do not have our racket prepared in the context that we have talked about with the previous shots, that is with your racket hand at shoulder level. On the forehand, your upper arm is behind your body in line with your shoulders and your racket hand is low at waist level.

You are often with your legs stretched out as you lunge forward or in a very low crouched position returning a difficult shot. It is better to be playing the lob off your front foot, so with your left leg forward on the right side of the court, and your right leg forward on the left side of the court. The truth is that getting to this difficult ball in the front of the court is the main priority so you can end up playing your lob with either your left or right foot out in front.

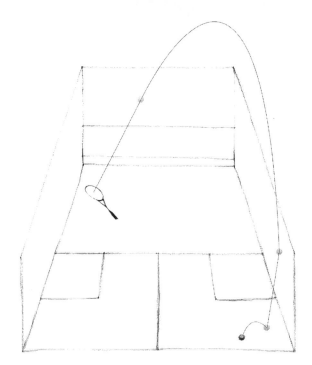

Lob shot line

Your target area on the front wall is about one metre above the service line with the objective of having the ball touch high on the side wall, behind the service box, before it is able to be hit. This will clearly limit your opponent's shot options.

Forehand lob body position   *Backhand lob body position*

You will need to get to the ball with your racket low and prepared, you hit underneath it and guide it gently upwards to the target area on the front wall so the ball floats high across the court. It should hit high on the sidewall and fall into the back corner.

The difference between the overhead forehand and backhand volley is worth thinking about when playing the lob. On the forehand almost everyone is able to volley the ball when it is high in the air. Most players have more power on the forehand side so it is very important that the lob is hit as high as possible and touches the side wall before your opponent is able to hit it.

I have seen that sometimes, after playing a lob, the player is 'surprised' because their opponent has played an attacking or winning shot. This is partly because they were relieved that they were able to return the difficult shot from the front of the court and relaxed. Do not relax after playing the lob, look immediately to see how good your lob was and then at your opponent. You will see immediately if your lob has limited their shot options or if they are preparing themselves to attack your lob. Obviously if you see early that they are going to attack your lob you will be better prepared to return the ball again.

Lobbing to your opponent's backhand is a very good defensive tactic. We are physically not able to hit the ball at the same height as we do on the forehand side. Neither do we have the same strength when we have to volley the ball high on the backhand side. By hitting a lob to your opponent's backhand, you are playing to a natural weak spot.

Practice routines

There are many different practice routines and they are generally all good for improving your game. The simple act of repeating shots in controlled conditions helps you to build habits that, with time, become part of your game. A lot of training is based around the idea that with more training hours and repeating the different shots in different routines you will improve your game. This is obviously quite true.

Having said that, I have occasionally heard players comment that they are bored with a particular routine. I have also seen them look for, and try, a different exercise in the hope that the new exercise may help them to improve their shots and game more quickly.

If there is a way to improve a little quicker, it is by focusing on the quality of your training. By this I do not mean, simply, that you should look to hit your target area more often. It is about using the controlled situation of the training exercise to build your awareness of ALL the details that are required to play each shot, every single time you hit the ball. Most routines are made up of only two or three different shots, so this allows you to focus on all the necessary details that are required for each shot.

Now I will go through some of the details that you can try and keep in mind during different practice routines. I can assure you that if you are constantly focused on all these details it is difficult to get bored even with the simplest of routines. They become a constant challenge where you are trying to improve your ability to put together and improve all the different movements that make up each shot. In essence it becomes a competition against yourself in which you are looking to understand and control your own body so that you are able to hit each shot with ever growing consistency. The more details that you are aware of and working on, automatically gives you more areas in which you can improve.

Boast and drive routine

This is probably the most commonly used exercise in squash. It is also an excellent exercise to start developing your consciousness of all details that make up hitting the ball well.

One player is in the front of the court and will hit the ball straight down the wall towards the back corner. The other player will only play boasts which means that both players will hit alternating forehand and backhand shots.

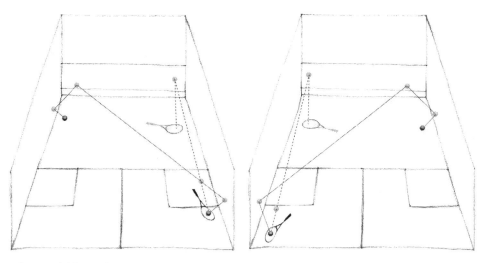

Boast and drive routine

The first objective is to hit the ball consistently well to your target area. To do this you need to hit the ball from the G Spot every time. Have your body in the best possible position for the shot you are going to play and have your racket back, prepared and stationary before hitting the ball.

When the player in the back of the court plays the boast, the player in the front starts preparing their racket, ensuring that it is back and ready to hit the ball before they get to the G Spot. You move directly to where you will hit the ball from with your racket back. In your last step to the ball turn your hips and shoulders so that they are parallel with the side wall and your feet are pointing to the side wall.

Your feet should be separated so that they are wider than your hips, but with the front foot slightly advanced because of the movement towards the ball. As discussed in the chapter 'Body position and feet', on the forehand the G Spot is in line with the shoulder of your racket arm so the ball is almost (but not quite) behind your body when you hit it. To have the ball in this position when you get to the ball, your last step to the ball should place your leading foot slightly in front of the ball so that it is in line with your racket shoulder when you hit it.

On the backhand side the G Spot is perpendicular to your front shoulder (of your racket arm) so between your front shoulder and the side wall when you get to the ball. You move directly to where you will hit from with your racket back. In your last step to the ball you turn your hips and shoulders so that they are parallel with the side wall and your feet pointing to the side wall. By putting together these details you can hit the ball as soon as you get to it.

At the same time, and before you get to the ball, you should have the target area clear in your mind. As I talked about earlier I prefer to have the ball bouncing in the back corner as the target area. I have seen that once players have the habit of hitting the ball clearly to the back corner they acquire the precision to hit it shorter when they need to or want to.

Look at the trajectory of the ball after it has hit the front wall. When you hit the drive well, the line of the ball after it has hit the front wall should curve in a slightly upwards direction before falling again in the back corner. This line of the ball allows you to hit the ball low and hard from the front of the court and at the same time ensure that the ball bounces in the back corner. Being aware of the way the ball moves off the front wall, and building the habit of hitting the ball in this way, will help you to be more conscious of how you can use the bounce of the ball off the front wall to your advantage. For example, sometimes hitting the ball in a flatter line so that it bounces for the second time just before it gets to the back wall will put your opponent under pressure if they are out of position.

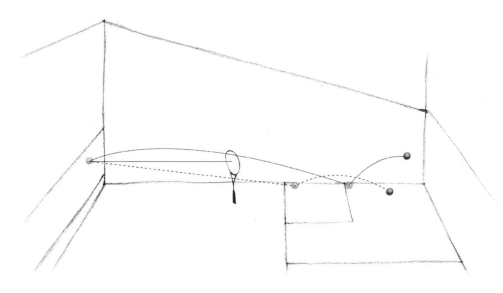

The two different ball trajectories when driving the ball

The ball should be as close as possible to the side wall moving straight down the side wall, ideally touching it halfway between the back of the service box and the back wall. Most courts have a lot of racket marks on the side wall in this area. Note that when the ball hits the side wall it slows slightly so it is better that it slows down in this area of the court.

When starting with this routine, I recommend that you give priority to having good body position, preparing your racket and hitting the ball from the G Spot, rather than feeling obliged to return to the T in between shots. Once you are consistently putting these details together and hitting the ball well, this is the moment to demand more of yourself and look to return to the T after each shot. Note that hitting your drive to the corner, so that your practice partner plays their boast after the ball has bounced off the back wall, will give you more time to return towards the T.

It is important that the player in the back of the court has a clear idea as to what boast they want to play. Either the boast that hits three walls, so in this case you are aiming for the ball to finish low on the side wall after it has hit the front wall or in the nick, or the boast that hits two walls so the ball bounces for the second time just before it hits the side wall at the front of the court. As I explained earlier,

I personally prefer to start with the three wall boast because it requires you to be able to place yourself at the limit of the range of the body positions that can be used for a boast.

The player who is boasting the ball starts to prepare his racket for the boast as soon as his practice partner hits their drive. He moves from the middle of the court to the back corner, arriving facing the back corner so that his shoulders are pointing at the side wall. He needs to have his racket back, prepared and stationary, feet should be separated with weight evenly placed on both feet. This allows him to adjust body position quickly to where he needs to hit the ball from and allows him to react instantly if the ball does not bounce the way he expects it to, as it occasionally does in the back corners.

The racket preparation is very important in the back corners because you often have very little time or space to hit the ball. This allows you to hit the ball at the first opportunity you have by simply moving your racket from the prepared position down behind and below the ball.

You can then look to vary the type of boast according to the quality of the drive your practice partner has played. For example, when they have hit a full length drive, and you are playing the boast after the ball has hit the back wall, hit the three wall boast. When they have hit a shorter length drive and you can hit the ball before it touches the back wall you can sometimes play the two wall boast. Look to see how they return this shot, have you forced them to move faster? Have they hit ball with the same precision? Have they prepared their racket early enough? This is the kind of awareness you can be developing while doing this simple routine.

As this routine has you playing forehand then backhand shots consecutively, you can increase the awareness of your racket preparation by having just two racket movements throughout the exercise. When you have finished your forehand drive or boast, your racket should have finished up by your other shoulder, which is basically where your racket should be when it is prepared for hitting your backhand shots. Leave it in this position and move to the backhand side of the court for your next shot. This is obviously exaggerating the time your racket is prepared but it can help you to become more aware of your racket preparation. In a game situation you would only start to prepare your racket once your opponent has hit the ball and you know from which side of the court you will be returning their shot from.

Note that I have given a very detailed explanation of this simple routine in the hope that you will be able to slowly improve your consciousness of what is required to hit the ball consistently better. I have not gone into so much detail when talking about the following routines but this does not mean they require less attention to detail. The same principles should be applied to all practice routines, focusing on the specific details that make up each shot.

Two drives and a boast routine

The first player plays a boast to the front forehand corner of the court. The second player plays a length shot to the back of the court. The first player then plays another drive to the back of the court. The second player moves to the back of the court and plays a boast to the front backhand corner. The first player then plays a drive to the back of the court. The routine then follows this sequence of two drives and one boast.

Pay attention to the length shots in this routine. For example, if your practice partner plays a shorter length from the front of the court, you should attack it with a dying length. This forces them to move faster and hit the ball before it bounces for a second time in the back of the court. If they have played a good length shot, you should ensure that your drive touches the back wall before they can hit it. This allows you more time to move to the front of the court to return their boast. Attention to these kind of details will help you to choose the best length shot option in your matches.

In all the practice routines you should be taking advantage of knowing where the ball is going to and work on your racket preparation, body position and hitting the ball from the G Spot.

Boast lob volley routine

This routine has both players moving diagonally from the back corner to the opposite front corner. The first player hits a boast and the second player moves to the front of the court with their racket prepared. As soon as they get to the ball they play their lob sending the ball to the front wall just above the service line so that it then hits high on the side wall behind the service box.

The first player then plays a volley straight down the side wall. If it is a good lob, and they can only hit the ball after it has touched the side wall, they should play the ball so that it bounces in the back corner. If they are able to volley the lob comfortably they should play the overhead volley 'smash', aiming so that the ball bounces for the second time just before the back wall.

The second player then plays a boast and the first player moves to the front of the court to play their lob. In this way both players are practicing all three shots.

When you are volleying the ball in this exercise it is important that you take advantage of the time you have. Ensure that your racket is prepared and that you have a good body position so that you can hit the ball at the G Spot.

Routines with drop shots

1. A simple routine to practice drop shots starts with one player in the front of the court and the second player in the back of the court. The player at the back of the court plays a boast to the front of the court. The player in the front then plays a drop shot, they then return their own drop shot by playing a straight drive to the back of the court. The player in the back of the court plays another straight drive to themselves in the back of the court and then plays a boast so that the player in the front can repeat the sequence.

You will be playing the drop shot in a situation that simulates a game situation with the advantage of knowing where the ball is being played to and the advantage of not having to move as far to get the ball. It is important that you use this conditioned situation to prepare well for your drop shot.

As soon as the player in the back of the court plays the boast you start moving to the front corner to where you will be playing the drop shot, preparing your racket as you move forward. In the last step to the ball ensure that you have turned your hips and shoulders to face the side wall and your feet are separated so that you have a good, stable body position. Remember that on the forehand side, to hit the ball from the G Spot, your last step should place your leading foot slightly in front of the ball.

Ensure that your racket is back, prepared and stationary when you get to the ball. Then hit the ball when it is at the G Spot so that it moves gently in a straight line to the target area, 10 centimetres above the tin on the front wall, and stays close to the side wall.

It is important that you move your body into a position so that you are hitting the ball at the top of the bounce.

After playing the drop shot you move forward and hit the ball again, driving it to the back corner. This will be difficult if your drop shot is good. Do not hit the drop shot so that you are able to return the drive comfortably. Focus on playing a good drop shot and if you cannot return the drive well give yourself a pat on the back. If necessary, pick up the ball and restart the routine by hitting the ball to the back of the court.

The player in the back of the court has plenty of time to prepare their racket and body position. When the ball comes to them in the back corner, they play a straight drive back to themselves. A simple way to be more precise is by defining where you play your drive to in the back of the court according to the type of length your practice partner has hit. If you can hit their length shot comfortably before it has hit the back wall, play a dying length that bounces for the second time just before the ball hits the back wall. If your practice partners drive has bounced off the back wall, you can return your drive to the back corner.

After you have played the drive back to yourself, hit the ball again and, play a boast so that your practice partner can repeat the sequence of a drop shot and then a drive.

2. Boast, drop shot, drive is another routine. It is more physically demanding and will test your stroke play. The first player plays a drive to the back of the court, the second player plays a boast, the first player moves to the front of the court

and plays a drop shot. The second player also moves to the front of the court to return the drop shot with a drive to the back of the court. The first player moves to the back corner and plays a boast. The exercise continues in this way with players alternating shots.

In this routine you are constantly moving quickly from corner to corner so it is a good opportunity to further develop your racket preparation and body position awareness. Be sure to start preparing your racket as soon as your practice partner plays their shot, ensuring that it is prepared and stationary before you hit each shot. Work on turning your hips and shoulders into the right position on your last step to the ball for each shot.

When playing the drop shot your first objective should be to ensure that you do not hit the tin. When your practice partner plays a good boast that is more difficult to return, aim to hit your drop shot a little higher. When their boast allows you a little more time, you can aim to be more precise with your drop shot, hitting it a little lower and ensuring that the ball stays very close to the side wall.

Volleying routines

1. A routine to practice volleying from the back of the court. Both players stand at the back of the service box, one on each side of the court. The players hit

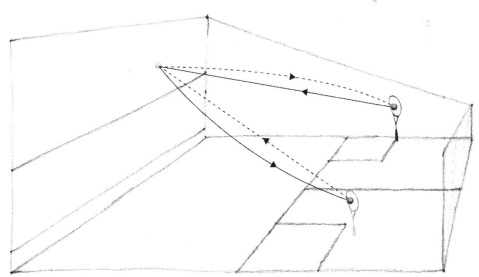

Back court cross court volley routine

high crosscourt volleys back and forth to one another. The objective for each player is to have their volley hit the side wall before their practice partner can volley it.

Both players are aiming to hit the ball high in the middle of the front wall. They should also be waiting for the ball with their rackets prepared. It is important they move both feet, taking their body to where they will hit the ball from. I have sometimes seen players doing this routine and their feet look like they are glued to the floor!

You can add to this routine a high straight volley by hitting the ball back to yourself. You then hit the ball again, returning a high crosscourt volley to your practice partner, who will then do the same.

Remember that you are practicing to improve your own volley and not just hitting volleys so that your practice partner can return them. Having said this, it may be necessary to hit easier volleys to one another at the beginning of this exercise so that you both get the rhythm of the routine. Practice for the same amount of time on each side of the court.

2. A routine to practice volley drop shots. Both players stand on the midcourt line facing the front wall, one on the forehand side and the other on the backhand side of the court.

The first player hits a medium speed crosscourt shot that is between hip and shoulder height. The second player plays a straight volley drop shot to the front corner and then moves forward and returns the same medium speed crosscourt shot to the first player. Repeat the same sequence, first a volley drop shot and then move forward and repeat the cross court shot.

It is very difficult to clearly identify the G Spot with this exercise because of the speed of the ball. You have very little time to turn your body to be parallel with the side wall so it is your racket preparation that will determine if you are able to play your volley drop shot consistently well.

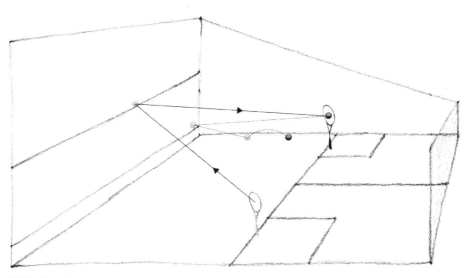

Volley drop shot routine

You need to ensure you have your racket prepared, with your upper arm in line with your shoulders on the forehand and on the backhand with your upper arm and elbow close to your body and your racket hand at the height of your other shoulder. It is important that your racket is stationary so that you only have to move it forward to the ball when you hit it. The face of your racket should be open. If you don't have time to turn your body to face the side wall, try and compensate for this lack of time by turning your shoulders as much as you can to face the side wall.

You move your racket behind and through to the ball hitting it firmly, but not hard, in a straight line to the front corner. The racket follow through should be the same as with the other shots but shorter as you are not hitting the ball hard. If your racket is finishing down at hip level, you could be cutting the ball. If you are cutting the ball it is more difficult to be consistent with your volley drop shots.

Your target area is about 10 centimetres above the tin. After the ball has hit the front wall you have two options. Firstly, aim for the ball to bounce on the floor and then stay close to the side wall or, secondly, you can aim for it to touch the side wall before it bounces on the floor. Remember the ball loses speed and bounces less when it touches the wall. Look at how the ball bounces in each case and decide which option you prefer so that you have a clear objective when hitting the ball.

Solo practice

Practicing alone is an excellent way to improve your ball control and racket awareness. I have heard players comment that hitting the ball alone on a squash court is boring. I have noticed that once you give yourself specific objectives for your body position, racket preparation and swing etc, the boredom disappears. Training alone can be an important and stimulating part of your squash evolution.

Being alone on the court has the advantage that you can focus on yourself. How you are moving your feet, your body position, your racket preparation and movement. You can also focus on the target areas on the front wall, where the ball bounces and the speed at which you hit the ball.

The following are some training exercises that have helped players improve their squash.

1. Hitting length. Stand in the back corner with your racket back and stationary, hit the ball just above the service line so that it returns to the back corner and bounces on the floor just before hitting the back wall. Repeat the same length shot to the back of the court. Aim to keep the ball as close as possible to the side wall. Ideally the ball should touch the side wall just behind the service box.

Every time you hit the ball you should move both feet to be sure you have the correct position. This simple correction or adjustment of the position of both feet allows you to have a good, balanced base to hit the ball from. Even if the ball comes back to the same place where you have just hit the ball from, move your feet a little. Your racket should already be back and prepared while you are moving your body into position. Focus on hitting the ball when it is at the G Spot. In the moment you hit the ball, be sure to transfer your weight from the back foot onto the front foot.

Vary the speed of your stroke between medium and high speed. You can alternate the speed with each shot, hitting the first ball hard and then the next ball slower. It is better if you vary the speed according to how well you are able to prepare the drive. If the ball is difficult to get out of the back corner or if it is very close to the wall, return it slower and higher. If you can return it comfortably, hit the ball harder.

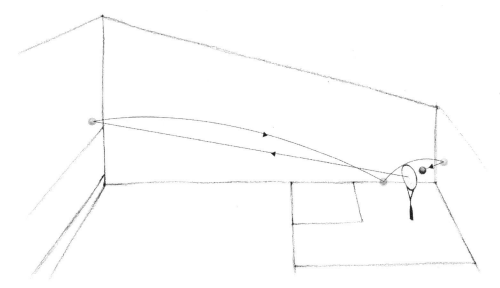

Hitting length solo line

If the ball bounces short of your target area (the back corner), make a clear effort to return the next shot to the back corner. Giving a small detail like this more importance when you are training can help with your mental approach in matches. Firstly you are doing a quality control on your training and then you are correcting yourself immediately when you have not hit your target area. By doing this kind of quality control in training, it will, in time, become a habit in match situations. It will also help you to more clearly identify when your opponent has played a shot that you can take advantage of.

Once you have practiced this routine and are able to do it with a reasonable rhythm you can add the option of a dying length. Choose a ball that allows you to prepare yourself with a good body position and then aim to hit the ball a little lower on the front wall and very hard. The objective is that the ball bounces for the second time, just before it touches the back wall. You then return this dying length again to the back corner. Play one or two more drives to the back corner and then play another dying length.

2. Front corner routine or 'eight drill'. Stand on the T and hit a forehand shot firmly to the front backhand corner, hitting the front wall first and then the side wall so that the ball returns to you. You then play a backhand firmly to the front forehand corner hitting the front wall and then the side wall so that the ball again returns to the T and you repeat the shot to the backhand front corner again. You then continue hitting the ball, alternating to the forehand and then the backhand front corners.

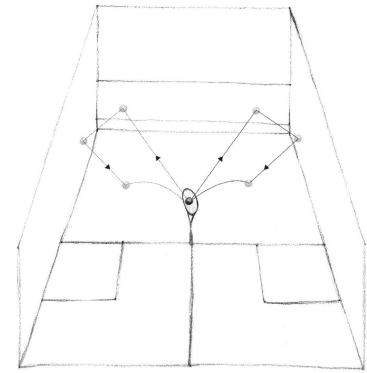

Eight drill line

This is a good routine to develop your racket preparation awareness. The ball comes back to you quite quickly so you don't have a lot of time to play the next shot. If your racket preparation is slow or late you will have trouble doing this exercise comfortably. It also helps you to develop the habit of a fluid, natural racket swing which is important for improving your front court game.

When you play the forehand shot, the racket follow through should finish up by your other shoulder. This is close to what should be the prepared position for your backhand shot so leave your racket there, stationary, so that when the ball returns from the front corner your racket is prepared and you can play your backhand shot immediately.

Your backhand swing follow through should finish with your upper arm and forearm in line with your shoulders. This is again close to the prepared position for the forehand shot so leave your racket there, stationary. When the ball returns from the front corner your racket is prepared and you can then play your forehand shot immediately.

For both forehand and backhand shots ensure your racket moves behind and through to the ball with an open racket face. Following this process you should end up with two simple racket movements that can help you hit the ball more precisely from the G Spot.

It is also important that you move your feet so that you have a good body position, with your shoulders aiming at the target area each time you hit the ball. As soon as you have played and completed the forehand shot you should move your body into position for the backhand shot.

The objective is to have four defined and separate movements when doing this routine:
1. The forehand swing hitting the ball.
2. Moving your body to the backhand position.
3. The backhand swing hitting the ball.
4. Moving your body to the forehand position.

I emphasise the above points because I have seen many players mixing them all together so they are moving their bodies at the same time as they are finishing their racket swings, or viceversa, so that they are in constant movement. I have also seen that it is quite common for some players not to move their feet at all when doing this kind of exercise. You will gain more from your practice session if you pay attention to these details.

Once you are comfortable with this routine, you can vary the speed and start hitting the ball harder. You can also start to add some variations that will help your front court game. For example, after you have hit three or four balls around the corners you can then play a drop shot. After you have played the forehand shot to the front, and the ball has returned to the T, you can play a backhand drop shot to the front backhand corner. This requires you to work a little harder, moving your body into the right position for the drop shot and, at the same time, helps you to create habits that you need in game situations. Be sure that the drop shot hits the front wall then the side wall, so that the ball returns to you at the T and you don't lose the rhythm of the routine.

When you start to add variations to this routine I recommend that, when you decide that the next shot will be the drop shot, you feed yourself the ball a little higher and softer so that you can prepare yourself for that shot. You then play three or four more shots around the front corners before you play another drop shot. At the beginning, try and play the forehand drop shots to the front forehand corner and the backhand drop shots to the front backhand corner. The easy option is to play crosscourt drop shots.

3. Front corners volley or 'eight routine'. This volley routine has the same principles as the eight drill, where the ball bounces before you hit it. Stand on the T and hit a forehand firmly to the front backhand corner, between one and two metres above the service line, hitting the front wall first and then the side wall so that the ball returns to you. Then play a backhand firmly to the front forehand corner, again between one and two metres above the service line, hitting the front wall first and then the side wall so that the ball again returns to the T and you can repeat the shot to the backhand front corner. You then continue hitting the ball, alternating to the forehand and then the backhand front corners.

The ball comes back to you quite quickly, so if your racket preparation is slow or late you will have trouble doing this exercise comfortably.

When you play the forehand shot, the racket follow through should finish up by your other shoulder. This is close to what should be the prepared position for your backhand shot, so leave your racket there and stationary. This way, when the ball returns from the front corner, your racket is prepared and you will be able to play your backhand volley immediately.

The follow through of the backhand swing should finish with your upper arm and forearm in line with your shoulders, which is close to the prepared position for the forehand shot. Leave your racket there, stationary, so that when the ball returns from the front corner your racket is prepared and you will be able to play your forehand volley immediately.

For both forehand and backhand shots ensure the racket moves behind and through the ball. Following this process you should end up with two simple racket movements that can help you hit the ball more precisely from the G Spot.

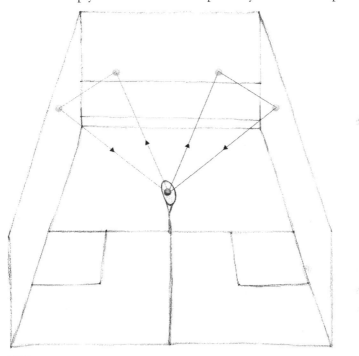

Volley eight drill line

It is also important that you move your feet so that you have a good body position, with your shoulders aiming at the target area. As soon as you have played and finished the forehand shot you should move your body into position for the backhand shot.

Once you are comfortable with this routine you can vary the speed, hitting the ball harder and a little lower on the front wall, or softer and higher, hitting the ball close to the outofcourt line.

You can then also add some variation by hitting volley kill shots or nick shots. After you have hit three or four volleys around the corners you can then play a volley to the front corner, first hitting the front wall and then the side wall. Practice both crosscourt and straight volleys to the front of the court.

Have a look at Victor Monserrat on YouTube, it is an example of the level of racket skill that can be achieved by practicing this kind of routine. *"Squash: Voleas 4 esquinas" http://youtu.be/loBpCWYPbiw*

4. Crosscourt volley nicks. Strangely, over the years I have seen that players love to try and play this shot in their matches yet they do not practice it very much. This is an easy shot to practice by yourself. Stand just behind the half court line then hit the ball high and straight back to yourself. Then turn your body so your shoulders are aimed across court, prepare your racket so that it is back and stationary, with a good balanced position and your weight spread evenly over both feet. Hit the ball firmly with a slightly open racket face to the front wall, about a metre from the front corner. The ball should then hit in the nick or low on the side wall before it bounces so that it stays low and is difficult to return. The routine will have continuity if you ensure the ball hits the side wall as the ball will return to where you hit the ball from.

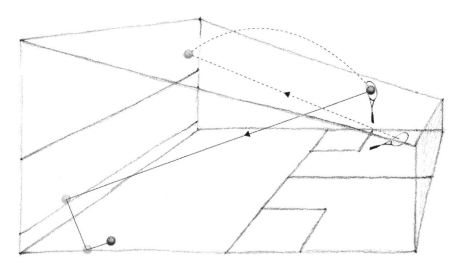

Cross court volley nick line

Conditioned games

These are games that you play with a practice partner in which you are limited to hitting the ball to specific areas of the court or only playing specific shots. They help you to create good playing habits that then become part your game. There are various conditioned games, here are a couple. Remember that it is how you play the game and not the game itself that will improve your squash.

1. Length game. This is a game that starts with a normal serve and then both players only hit the ball to the back of the court. There are two options, either having all the shots bouncing behind the service box or having all the shots bounce behind the midcourt line. I recommend that you experiment with both options. Quite simply, when one of the players hits the ball short of the agreed target area, they lose the point.

Hitting the ball behind the service box is the more difficult option and the points will be shorter. After playing this game a few times you will start to recognise the shots that may be difficult to hit out of the back corner and you will start to try and hit or volley the ball earlier.

Hitting the ball behind the midcourt line is a little easier and the points will be longer. This option gives you the chance to experiment with the two different types of length. Start with a full length to the back corner and then, as soon as you are able, hit the ball with a good body position, with your racket prepared etc., hit the ball very hard to a dying length. A general rule when playing length games is that when you have difficulty returning your practice partner's shots, you should try and hit a full length to the back corner and if you can hit their shot comfortably, attack it by playing the dying length.

You should look to clearly define which one of the length options you are going to play every time you hit the ball and not just be happy if the ball passes over the midcourt line.

With both length games it is important to be looking to volley as much as possible. You know that the ball is coming to the back of the court so, as soon as your opponent hits the ball, you should be looking to see if you will have the opportunity to volley the ball. This will help you to volley more in match situations.

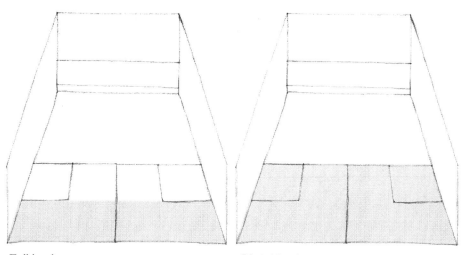

Full length game zone   *Varied length game zone*

2. Side court or alley game. In this game you can only play on the forehand or backhand side of the court. You draw an imaginary line from the back of the court to the front of the court that follows the width of the service box. The ball must bounce between this imaginary line and the side wall. Both players can hit the ball anywhere within this area. When the ball bounces outside this area, the player who has hit the ball out loses that point. Play a complete game using one side of the court and then play another game on the other side of the court.

Start the game with a normal serve and then both players must hit every shot within this reduced area. It is difficult to play winning shots because both players know which side of the court the ball will be on, so it is important to focus on not making mistakes. You should try to keep the ball as close as possible to the side wall.

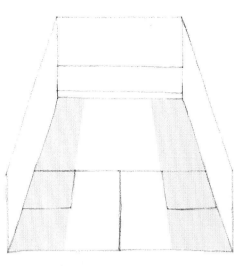

Alley game zones

This alley game is a good opportunity to work on your racket preparation and hitting the ball at the G Spot. Quite simply, after you have played each shot you can return your racket to the prepared position and then move to your next shot. This simple exercise can help you develop and improve your racket awareness.

Tactics

Squash is a very tactical game played at high speed in a reduced space. It is the sum of a series of details and understanding those details that will be the difference between winning and losing matches.

It is an attacking game and a defensive game, it is about recognising the right time to play attacking shots and the right time to play defensive shots. It is about putting pressure on your opponent and about survival when you are under pressure.

Squash is a game of rallies where points are won and lost as much through good shots as from your mistakes or your opponent's mistakes.

Tactics in squash have always been quite clear. Simple concepts like making your opponent run more than yourself, controlling the T, keeping your opponent in the back of the court, playing to the front of the court when your opponent is behind you, and keeping the ball as close as possible to the side walls are your tactical objectives. They are all correct and important. However, do not prioritise any of them. It is the interrelationship of these concepts and using them all together that can make the difference.

When talking about wearing your opponent out by making them run more often brings to mind the idea of them running from the back corner of the court diagonally to the opposite front corner of the court because it is the longest distance within a squash court. It is very difficult to move your opponent constantly from the back to the front of the court and is not always the best way to move your opponent. The difference is often a lot more subtle.

I liken it to two people of equal fitness going for a long run side by side around a 400 metre track. After 15 minutes they are both running comfortably. After 30 minutes the runner on the outside of the track is starting to breathe a little heavier than the runner on the inside. After 45 minutes the runner on the outside is having trouble keeping up with his training partner. After 60 minutes the runner on the outside can no longer run at the same speed as his training partner and stops running. The reality is that, without realising it, the runner on the outside of the track has run a few hundred metres more than his companion because, each time he has completed another 400 metres, he has run extra.

This idea of small differences in distance accumulating over the duration of a match is often the difference between winning and losing. In squash it is very difficult to measure who has covered more metres in a match, but in the end it is about having your opponent move an extra metre or two than you in each rally.

This difference is very difficult to see in the context of one rally and often goes unnoticed. I have found that to become more conscious of these subtle details it is better to focus on where your opponent is returning your shot from. This may appear to very obvious but I have seen that many players are just focused on their own shot and, if they have hit it in the general direction they were aiming for, they are happy. They then wait for their next turn to hit the ball.

The grey zone

A way of building this awareness is to have a clear idea in your mind about the area where you do not want your opponent to be hitting the ball from. For example, create a 'grey zone' in the middle of the court from the back of the service boxes to one metre in front of the midcourt line, and be clear that you do not want your opponent hitting the ball from this area. Having this clear in your mind helps you maintain a quality control over your own shots. By recognising immediately when your opponent is hitting the ball in this grey area, you can correct the situation with your next shot. Being aware of this also helps you to see that you have a slight advantage in the moment you are hitting the ball from the grey zone and, if your next shot keeps your opponent out of this area, your opponent will be moving an extra metre or more.

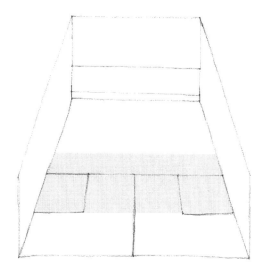

The grey zone

In squash we spend more time playing to and from the back of the court than we do in the front of the court. Being able to build up small differences in the amount of extra metres your opponent moves in the back of the court can be decisive.

When your opponent is behind you and has hit a weaker shot, it is apparently the obvious moment to move them by hitting the ball to the front corner of the court. Be careful with this simple tactic. After playing a weak shot most players prepare themselves to return to the T and to the front of the court as fast as they can. Sometimes the momentum they have from moving fast to the front allows them to return an attacking shot with extra energy. If you hit the first one or two weak shots they play to the back of the court, your opponent will hesitate before moving forward. This tactic can reduce your opponent's momentum, thus making your shot to the front of the court more effective. It is important that you use the extra time you have, because of your opponent's weak shot, to ensure you hit a good dying length out of the grey area otherwise you will lose the advantage you have gained.

Having your opponent run more is not the only way to tire them. Given the speed of squash there are other factors that require a lot of energy. They are the constant stopping, starting and changing of direction that are a part of every point in a game of squash.

One of the most tiring movements is to return to the same corner from where you have just hit the ball from after having played a weaker shot.

When you have hit the weak shot, you immediately realise that you must move quickly if you are to have a chance of recovering and move as quick as you can towards the T. If your opponent then hits the ball to the same back corner you have just moved out of, you have to stop instantly, turn 180 degrees and return. These stopping, turning and starting movements use a lot of energy.

If you use this tactic to tire your opponent, you must be 100% sure that your opponent returns to the back corner, otherwise you may be gifting them with a shot that allows them to recover in the point.

Attacking and defending

In squash you are constantly changing from attacking to defensive situations, often within the same rally. It is important to remember that whether you attack or defend depends on a combination of your own play and that of your opponents. Your attacking play can force your opponent to defend and their defensive play and counter attacking can then force you into defensive situations.

There are various ways of playing attacking squash; hitting the ball very hard and fast, constantly hitting the ball as early as possible, volleying a lot, controlling the T, playing attacking shots to the front of the court, keeping the ball very close to the walls and moving your opponent all over the court. In reality you should be trying to do all of these things, they are all important and you should be trying to do them all in the right moment. All of these details will be more effective if you force your opponents to play their shots from outside the grey area.

When do you attack? You can attack when you are able to get to the ball and have time to prepare your shot. Being aware of your racket preparation and body position can help you to see clearly the right moment for an attacking shot. Make a conscious effort to hit the ball hard, the speed of the ball forces your opponent to move faster and they will have less time to prepare and play their next shot.

The next factor is if you are able to play your shot from within the grey area. You have to move a short distance to the ball from the T and your objective should be to ensure that your opponent plays their next shot from outside the grey area, either from the back of the court or from the front of the court.

Controlling the T and volleying a lot are very much interrelated. If you are on the T you will have more opportunities to volley. Being able to get to the T after every shot depends on the time you have between shots and the speed at which you move. If you play long length drives to the back wall you can normally get to the T comfortably.

If you play dying length drives you can get back to the T using your speed, although it depends a little on where you have played your shot from. If you play the dying length drive from the grey area you will be able to return to the T. When you play the dying length from the back of the court it is more difficult to get to the T.

If you constantly hit the ball to the grey area, you need to be superman or superwoman to be able to return to the T after each shot for a whole match. Getting to the T and controlling it depends on your own speed and where you hit the ball.

People associate attacking squash with volleying to the front of the court. In reality, most volleys should be considered attacking squash because, by volleying, you are giving your opponent less time to play their next shot and return to the T. Players who volley a lot are normally those who are watching their opponents closely as they are hitting the ball. They see immediately where the ball is going. If it is hit high on the front wall, they start preparing themselves immediately because they may have the opportunity to volley. You should be constantly looking or hunting for opportunities to volley. This is part of an attacking mentality.

Hitting the ball hard and fast is the most common form of attacking squash. Your opponent has less time to get to the ball and hit it. It tires them and when they are under pressure they will make mistakes. The only problem with hitting the ball very hard is that sometimes players become less accurate and are not focused on a target area. It is the combination of speed, ensuring your opponent is not returning your shot from within the grey area, and keeping the ball close to the side wall that gives you the maximum benefit from hitting the ball hard. Try and have all three factors in mind when playing your shot.

When should you play defensively? Identifying the moment or situation in which you should play defensively and having a clear idea of what shot you should play is an important part of squash tactics.

The most obvious defensive situation is when you are struggling to get to the ball either at the front or the back of the court. Your main objective here should be to ensure that your shot forces your opponent to the back of the court and, if possible, that they hit the ball after it bounces off the back wall. This will give you the maximum amount of time to recover your position in the court.

When in a defensive situation at the front of the court you need to be aware that your opponent may be looking to volley your shot so you need to hit the ball hard and try to keep it close to the side wall. Another option is to play a lob. The lob reduces the speed of the ball so you also gain a little more time. Remember that lobbing the ball to your opponent's backhand is an excellent defensive shot.

Playing a drop shot when in a defensive situation is normally quite risky. Sometimes you have no option because you are extremely stretched when getting to the ball, or the ball is close to the side wall. Focus on playing a straight drop shot, trying to keep the ball as close as possible to the side wall. A cross drop shot is normally a bad defensive option because your opponent will have easy access to the ball and an open court. If they hit the ball straight down the wall, you'll have a long way to run if you are to return it. By playing a straight drop shot your opponent has to move around your body to get to the ball. It is a little more difficult for them to get to it quickly and you are in a better position to see where they want to hit it to.

The defensive drop shot works better if you have been regularly hitting the ball to the back of the court, because then your opponent is not expecting you to play a drop shot.

When defending in the back of the court your objective is to return the ball to the back corner again so you have time to recover and get back to the T. When you are under pressure it is often better to hit the ball at a medium pace with the objective of being more accurate. Hit the ball above the service line using the height of the ball to ensure that it returns to the back corner. It is better to play a straight drive, aiming for the ball to stay as close as possible to the side wall.

When in a defensive situation at the back of the court, players are often tempted to hit the ball high and crosscourt hoping that their opponent is not expecting this shot. If you do not ensure that the ball touches the side wall before they are able to hit it, you will give your opponent an easy volley. For this reason I recommend that you play your recovery shots mainly straight down the wall. Being clear in your own mind which shot you need to play is the first step to improving your defensive play. Then, by constantly repeating the same shot, you will slowly improve its quality, getting it deeper into the corner and closer to the wall. People can say that if you always play the same shot your opponent will be expecting it. In reply to this I would say that your objective is to play the defensive straight drive consistently well so that even if they know where you will hit the ball, they will not be able to volley it and will be forced to return to the back corner to play their next shot. When you see that they are anticipating your straight drive, the high crosscourt variation then becomes a good shot to play. Play the high crosscourt shot once or twice and then return to playing the straight drives again.

Occasionally in a rally you can find yourself in a situation where your opponent has gained complete control. They have you constantly running around the court, you are struggling to return the ball and cannot get back to the T. Sometimes this happens if you have momentarily lost your concentration. As soon as you realise you have lost control, you need to focus on recovering and stop the dynamics of this point. The solution is simple. Hit the ball to the back of the court so that you gain time between shots. You need to hit the ball there at least two or three times so the rally calms down a little and you are able to recover. If you manage to do this, you may even frustrate your opponent and gain a slight psychological advantage because they had expected to win the point after moving you all around the court.

After having chased the ball around the court and surviving in the rally, there is sometimes the temptation to try and win the point at the first opportunity you have to hit the ball comfortably. It looks good and is a great feeling if you manage to do it, but I have seen that more players lose the point in this situation than they win it. Your body is full of adrenalin because of your fight to survive, thus making it difficult to have the necessary calm to play a winning shot. Being aware of this may help you to choose the right shot.

Speed variation

As squash has evolved over the years it has become fitness and speed oriented. In reality, hitting the ball hard and moving as fast as you can is one of the main challenges and pleasures of playing squash for many players. This has led to players using less variety in their games.

Changing the speed of the ball can upset the rhythm of your opponent and cause them to make 'unforced' errors. How many times have you or your opponents missed a supposedly easy shot? Part of the reason for missing this shot is because the easy ball has come to you at a different speed, normally slower.

Hitting the ball harder than normal can also cause your opponent to make mistakes because they have to move faster to the ball and have less time to hit it.

In both cases it can be the change of rhythm more than the simple fact that you have hit the ball harder or softer that causes the mistake. Most players have a speed they are comfortable playing at. Try and recognise this speed and then test them with faster or slower balls. Remember to vary the speed in every game. As games evolve, the changes of rhythm can become more effective.

Slowing the ball down is also an important tool when you need to recover after a difficult point. Hitting the ball slower gives you more time between every shot. You will only recover if you hit the ball slower and to the back of the court at various times.

Be careful though, as sometimes when players slow the speed of the ball they also hit the ball shorter in the court. Remember that irrespective of the speed you hit the ball, you do not want your opponent hitting the ball in the grey area.

Deception

It's a great feeling when you hit the ball somewhere in the court and your opponent moves in a different direction, only to find that the ball is not where they expected it to be. Deception is not a tactic. It is a variation that you can occasionally include in your game. Winning matches cannot be based on deceptive play. Yet, you can win a point with a deceptive shot.

There are two ways of playing a deceptive shot. One is by changing the direction of where you hit the ball at last moment. The second is when, after having constantly hit the ball to the same place in the court, you hit the ball somewhere else. For example, after hitting a straight backhand drive ten times from the grey area, you then hit the eleventh shot to the front of the court with a drop shot. Your opponent has the habit of moving to a straight drive, they then must correct themselves and move to where you have hit the ball.

Your body position is an important factor in deception. If your opponent sees clearly from your body position that you want to play a crosscourt shot and then you hit a straight ball, you can surprise them. By showing a clear body position and changing at the last moment where you hit the ball will make your deceptive shots more effective.

Mental fitness

I am certainly not qualified to talk about sports psychology. I have been fascinated by how a player's brain can interfere with their natural or instinctive body movements. Also, how a player's performance can change from one moment to the next for no apparent reason. The following observations are based on my personal experiences from playing and coaching.

When I was 16 or 17 years old, my mother occasionally commented to me after a match that I wasn't concentrating! I had no idea what she was talking about. I was just happy chasing the little black ball around the court. Concentration was a grey area that was often referred to, but there seemed to be very few specific tools or advice given to help improve it.

I have seen many players who were physically and/or technically superior to their opponents lose matches because their minds have interfered with their game. It is clear that this facet of squash needs special attention and that it can be improved with training, just like the other aspects that make up squash. The physical, tactical and technical areas are easier to see and understand so we tend to focus on them more.

It is very difficult to give a set of guidelines that will help players, because the mind of every individual works differently. Each player will need to find specific solutions for the areas where they are weaker.

Often our heads do not want to be responsible when things are going badly. We then blame our legs, our rackets, the courts, the referee etc. For example, if the referee awards a point against us, we disagree and sometimes get angry with them. Getting angry distracts us, then we do not play as well as we should and perhaps lose another point. Our head then tells us that the referee is to blame for this further loss. In reality it was our head that chose to play the wrong shot or was not paying enough attention when we were hitting the ball, so the ball came back too close to us and the referee was obliged to award a stroke to our opponent. We played the bad shot, it is almost never the referee's fault.

I coached a talented young player who was very fast around the court. Occasionally, when things were not going well, he would literally beat his legs with his racket complaining that they were not working properly. To me he appeared to be moving with his normal explosive speed. I realised later that the problem was that he was not concentrating properly therefore not moving to the ball, as he normally would, as soon as his opponent had played their shot. Instead, he was starting to move after the ball had hit the front wall. This meant that he was getting to the ball later than he normally would and consequently was uncomfortable hitting the ball. The more he blamed his legs, the worse things got for him. The reality was that he was not concentrating as well as he normally did.

When you put players of a similar physical level on the court to do court sprints there is normally very little time difference between them. When you put the same two players into a game situation there is often a player who is seen to be faster on the court.

Sprinting is principally a physical activity. Squash matches are physical and mental battles so this apparent difference in speed between the two players comes from the faster player being more focused on the ball and moving as soon as their opponent hits it. The faster player consciously or subconsciously starts to move to the forehand or backhand side as soon as they see which side of the court the ball has been hit to. At the same time, they define whether they have to move to the front, mid or back court areas. If the ball is going to the back of the court they look to see if they can volley the ball before it gets to the back wall. If that is not possible they then follow the ball to the back of the court and hit it from there.

The player who appears to be not quite as fast on the court, is maybe waiting until the ball has hit the front wall before they start moving to where they will hit it from. Their mind, or lack of attention, is limiting their speed.

So speed on the squash court is not purely physical. To be very fast you have to add the psychological factor of being constantly aware of what is happening on the court and reacting as soon as your opponent hits the ball.

Some people instinctively develop this kind of reaction. Others need to learn or develop them consciously. If a concept is logical, the mind says immediately "OK, I'll do that" and expects it to happen automatically. The reality is that, like your physical fitness, it takes time and constant work to get to develop the kind of reactions that will help you to attain a higher level of concentration. It can be done but you need time and patience to build them.

Winning

Most players go on to the court hoping to win the match. That's normal, but sometimes the desire or need to win becomes a distraction. If you are thinking too much about winning, you are not focused on the many details that you need to put together to play well. You win by hitting the ball to the right areas of the court.

I have seen that if you are focusing constantly on the small details, such as, your movement to the ball, your racket preparation and swing, hitting the ball at the G Spot, where you are going to hit the ball to etc., can help to improve your concentration. Working your mind on a shot-by-shot and then on a point-by-point basis helps to keep other possible distractions out of your mind.

Thoughts about winning during games can also complicate things. In evenly balanced games where you have managed to gain a slight advantage, having thoughts like "I'm winning!", "I could win this game" or "only 2 points to go" occasionally can cause a player to relax subconsciously. Add to this minimum relaxation the fact that your opponent, who has fallen behind on the score board, reacts and tends to fight a little more is a contributing factor as to the reason why players sometimes lose games they perhaps should have won. If you manage to get ahead and have these kind of thoughts, recognise immediately that they are dangerous and make an effort to return your focus to the details that have helped you gain the advantage. If possible, avoid thinking about winning points or games until you have finished the match.

I have also seen players complicate games that they should have won comfortably because they have started the match believing that they would win easily. Thinking that you should win easily sometimes causes a subconscious relaxation. This minimum relaxation can cause you to start the match less than 100% focused, so your general play is not at its usual level, which allows your opponent to feel more comfortable.

Susan Devoy almost never had this problem. I remember that even when she was clearly the best player in New Zealand she would sometimes comment before her first round match in a worried tone "I have heard that (whoever her who first round opponent was) is playing really well". This type of respect for your opponent, whoever they may be, or even a fear of losing unexpectedly, can help you to play at your best level so that you avoid 'surprise' results.

You should only think about winning easily after you have finished the match. Sometimes after winning comfortably people comment that you had an "easy win". Often the reality is that you are both physically and mentally tired. It requires a huge amount of energy to maintain focus on all the details that make up playing well.

Ghandi said the root of all problems is egoism. Egos in sport can be very complicated things. On one hand you should be satisfied and proud of your achievements. On the other hand, it is another thing to believe that you are a good player and project this to others. I have seen that sometimes when a person has a high impression of their own level, their ability to learn or see where they can improve becomes limited. It is almost as if their ego has partially blinded them to their own reality. This can occur at all levels, from club players through to professional players. There is always room to improve and learn. Your ability to see and accept your weaknesses is the first step towards finding solutions.

After losing a match players who enjoy the physical side of squash 'see' that they need to be stronger and fitter to win. Maybe their reality was that they were not hitting the ball to the right areas in the court or they need to work on how they hit the ball.

After losing, a player whose game is based on how well they hit the ball tends to 'see' that they need to practice their shots more and make less mistakes. Maybe their reality is that they need get fitter so that they are able to get to the ball better or improve their concentration.

We all have egos. It is a question of keeping it under control so that you can see the overall reality of your match results.

In a match your battle is as much with yourself as it is with your opponent. Your first objective is to take all your weapons to the court and then use them to your own advantage. The result then depends on a combination of factors that comes from both players. Seeing honestly this combination, and the factors that have contributed to the result, will help you to identify the areas of your game you need to work on.

Sometimes after losing a match players say that they have played badly. This could be true or was it that your opponent played very well? Do they simply have a different level to you? What were they doing that made it so that you were not able to play comfortably? Were there parts of the match in which you felt comfortable? Was this because you were doing something specific that limited their play? (Try and identify what you were doing.) Was it because they relaxed a little?

The two most common reasons for sudden changes in the level of your play are that you are not concentrating as you normally would or that you are tired, for example, from a previous match. It takes months to make noticeable changes in your technique or fitness so, by the same token, your level of play cannot change overnight either.

Answering these kind of questions without your ego's interference is not easy.

Shot options

One of the constant dilemmas squash gives us is "where should I hit the ball now?". In a match you rarely have a lot of time to decide where the best place to hit the ball is, and you are often in situations where you have multiple shot options. You have to decide quickly whether to hit the ball straight or crosscourt, to the front or to the back of the court.

Another type of thought that can come into your head when deciding where to hit the ball is, "let's see what happens if I try this shot" or "maybe they won't expect this shot". These thoughts are, in essence, good. The problem is when they become a habit and your choice of shot depends on them.

A way to improve your shot choices is to recognise the various specific situations that appear during rallies and identify what you believe to be the best option for that situation. You should then constantly play that shot. This helps you to develop and improve that specific shot which, in turn, will add more definition to your game. Following this idea, the next thought that comes to mind is that your opponent may see that you are repeating the same shot in a specific situation and knows where to go to return the ball. My reply to this fear is that it is generally better to play the right shot according to the situation even though your opponent may know where you will be hitting it to. Just concentrate on playing your shot well. This also means that variations from your chosen shot are then unexpected and more effective. If you are constantly experimenting with different shots, it is difficult to surprise your opponent.

It is important to remember that improving your mental fitness takes time. Most people already understand that it takes time to get physically fitter and stronger and that you achieve your physical goals by slowly increasing your workload as your body develops. Mental fitness is the same but you need to be aware of the need to develop your mental strength to take the first step towards improvement.

Every person's mind is different and has a unique way of working. Some people are calm, others are more tense or nervous, some are more serious, others are light-hearted etc. This means that the starting point is different for each person. It is like going into a labyrinth, you need to try all the different paths. Some paths will be a dead end and others will take you closer to the G Spot. You can learn something from every path, even if it is only not to go there again.

What is clear is that it is an ongoing building process that has no limits. Over time, you are slowly learning and adding new details to the mix of things that will help you perform better.

Nicol David said after winning the 2014 British Open "My ambition is not to win as many titles as I can. It's more about understanding myself through squash. It's a sport that has got so many aspects, every time I get on court, I learn something new all the time.".

Physical Fitness

The physical side of squash is probably the easiest part of squash to understand. It is one of the main reasons many people play squash. Very rarely do you play squash without getting a good workout. Playing regularly makes you fitter and, by getting fitter, your level of squash improves.

Squash fitness requires the resistance of a long distance runner, the speed and strength of a sprinter and an ability to recover quickly that few other sports demand of their participants.

Everyone knows what it feels like to be out of breath and tired after a hard match. It is something we can all relate to. For this reason many players appear to focus more on this area, giving it more importance than the technical, tactical and psychological parts of their game. It is important that you look for a healthy balance between these different parts of your game. They are all interrelated. If you are fit, you will get to the ball easier so you will be able hit the ball better. If you do not hit the ball very well, or if you hit it to the wrong part of the court, you will have to run more and you will tire quicker. If you are not concentrating you will lose points easily and then you will have to work harder to recover.

It is clear that to play squash very well, you need a high level of fitness. A high level of fitness can only be achieved over a long period of time with a lot of hard work and constant training. It is a slow building process where you first learn your body's limits and then, through training, you gradually push them upwards.

I have sometimes heard players saying that they have a tournament in two, three or four weeks so they need to train a lot for it. In this amount of time you can only fine-tune a little of your actual level of fitness. You cannot make noticeable changes in your level of fitness in this time. Players who prepare for tournaments in this way rarely win them.

To achieve noticeable differences in your fitness you need to have a longer-term vision and patience. Give yourself an objective of constant training for six months or a year. The first priority is to train regularly over this longer period. Then, once your body is acclimatised to the regular training, you should then slowly increase the volume of work. It is important that you do not compare yourself to others. Everyone is different and each person's starting point is different. Your fitness battle can only be with yourself.

Do not compare your evolution with how well you did or felt the previous day or the previous week. Changes in short periods of time are normally due to circumstantial conditions like; if you are more or less tired or if you are more or less focused on your training. Add to this that there may be external factors in your day-to-day life that influence how you feel while training. These changes in how you feel on a daily or weekly level are not an indication of changes in your level of fitness. They are part of the building process. If your head is asking questions like "is this effort really worthwhile?" or saying "I'm getting worse, not better" and you need to give yourself a boost, look at the level you were at three or even six months earlier. This comparison may help you to feel a little better and see that you are progressing in the right direction.

Ian McKenzie said to me when I first arrived in London from New Zealand that, to achieve really noticeable changes in your squash, you need to understand that you require at least three years of training and hard work. I have seen that this is generally right.

There are not many secrets to getting fitter. It can be done on and off the court. There are many fitness professionals with tried and proven systems. The interesting thing about these systems is that they are often quite different, while the objectives and results are similar. What they all have in common is the intensity and a consistency that is constantly pushing the player to their limits.

It is important to plan your training. Make a reasonable estimate of the time you have available. Within this time look for a balance that includes solo training, practice routines, games or matches and fitness training. Look at your weaknesses and include exercises that will help you to improve in these areas. It is more fun working on your strong points, but you will learn more by improving your weak points.

Plan for one hard or intense day followed by an easier day and repeat this pattern. Have one day off per week.

Include a mix of aerobic and anaerobic exercises. Aerobic exercise is, for example, road and hill running or cycling. You do these activities at a medium pace and for thirty minutes to one hour. Ensure that you start at a speed that allows you to complete your planned run or bike ride comfortably. If you can, increase the speed over the last five to ten minutes. This allows you to gauge your level. If you start too fast, you will get to your limit very early and then the rest of the run or bike ride is difficult and often painful (physically and/or psychologically). People who start too fast do not enjoy themselves and then sometimes lose interest in training. As you learn your limits, you increase the time and distance. Aerobic exercise is used more in pre-season training to build overall fitness.

Court sprints, athletic track running and circuit training are anaerobic exercises. These are extremely intense activities designed to push your body to its limits and to improve your mobility, strength and ability to recover physically after hard rallies. You do them in series for around one to two minutes.

Court sprints

There are many different variations of court sprints. Here are some of them.

Court lengths, you sprint 20, 22 or 24 lengths of the court (depending on your level of fitness), touching the floor at each end of the court. You then rest for a minute. You can also run for a minute and then rest for a minute. Start with four repetitions for example. As you get to know your limits and your body becomes conditioned to this type of exercise, you increase the number of repetitions. It is not uncommon for players to get up to 10 repetitions.

Ross Norman introduced me to a variation of this type of court sprint when I trained with him in London. He would do a series of 50 lengths of the court, touching the top of the tin on the front wall and touching the back wall at the same level. This is an extreme form of court sprints and should only be done if you already have a very good level of fitness. We used to build up to six series of 50 lengths with about one minute rest in between each series. The time to do the

50 lengths was between 2 minutes 10 seconds and 2 minutes 25 seconds. No one did it faster than Ross.

Quarter court sprints. You start at the back of the court. You move forward fast and touch the back line of the service box and return to the back wall, touching the floor (first quarter). You then move forward to touch the line at the front of the service box and again return to touch the floor by the back wall (two quarters). Then you sprint forward to the point halfway between the front of the service box and the front wall and return to touch the floor by the back wall (three quarters). You then sprint to the front wall and return to touch the floor by the back wall (four quarters). You then work backwards, doing again the four quarters, then three quarters, two quarters and the one quarter. You repeat the sequence, which will give you around a minute of intense exercise. You rest for a minute and then repeat the double sequence.

A variation of this quarter court sprint is to run backwards to the back wall after running to each quarter.

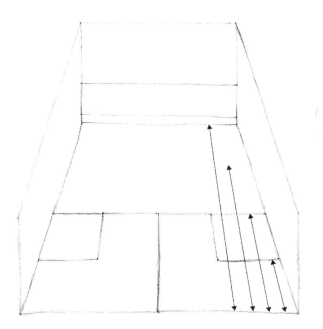

Quarter court sprints

Shadowing without the ball. This is an on-court sprint training that simulates a game situation. You start on the T and must return to the T after each movement. You move as fast as you can alternately to both front corners, both back corners and both side walls in the service box and you simulate hitting the ball before moving back to the T. During this exercise you can work on your racket preparation by preparing it as you move from the T and readying your body position by turning your hips and shoulders where you would normally be hitting the ball. You do this for one minute and then rest or recover for one minute before repeating the exercise.

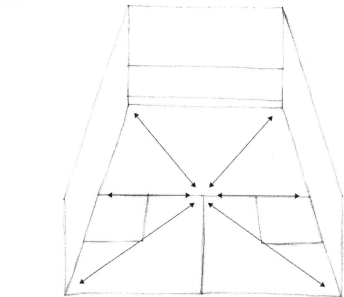

Shadowing court sprints

You can also do your shadow training by moving randomly to the different positions. The random shadowing can also be done with your practice partner. They stand in the middle of the court in front of the T and indicate where you have to run to as soon as you have returned to the T.

Shadowing with the ball. Gamal Awad showed me this exercise. One player stays in the front corner and can hit the ball wherever they want to. The other player must always return the ball to the front wall in the corner where their partner is. If the ball bounces twice or dies before you can hit it back to the front wall, you pick it up as quickly as you can and hit it back to the corner where your partner is.

Do this for two minutes and rest before repeating the exercise. (Gamal used to do series of four or five minutes with a short rest in between each series.)

The recovery times given above for each court sprint exercise are a general guide. Each person is different, some people may need a little more time and others may be ready to start sooner. Listen to your own body and work accordingly. You can also monitor your heart rate and use it as a guide to how long you rest between each series.

Track running

Training on the track has a similar objective to the court sprints and training outside is always nice. You are building your mobility, strength and improving your ability to recover. You do a series of 400, 500 or 600 metre runs as fast as you can. Start with four or five series of 400 metres. Get to know your level of fitness and then slowly build the number of series that you do. Again, you rest for around a minute between each run.

Circuit training

Circuit training is also a good way to improve mobility, strength and stamina. It comprises of six to ten strength exercises that are completed one exercise after another. Each exercise is performed for a specified number of repetitions or for a set time before moving on to the next exercise. The exercises within each circuit are separated by a short rest period, and each circuit is separated by a longer rest period. The total number of circuits performed during a training session may vary from two to six depending on your training level, your period of training (preparation or competition) and your training objective.

There are different web pages where you can get more specific information about planning your circuit training, a useful one is *www.brianmac.co.uk/circuit.htm*

Swimming and weight training can also be included in your training programme, as they develop your strength and offer balanced exercise that helps to compensate for the fact that, in squash, we tend to use one side of the body more than the other.

Stretching

Being flexible will help your squash. In matches you are constantly changing direction, stopping and starting as you chase the ball around the court. Stretching prepares your body for this kind of intense movement and will help you to avoid injuries.

Stretching is very easy to do. You can do it almost anywhere and it does not require a lot of space or time. Stretching for a minute while you are waiting for a train or for thirty minutes while watching TV , for example, is good for you.

Stretching must be an integral part of your training programme. There are many specialised books on the subject. It is good to learn about the many different stretching exercises and experience them for yourself. Take note of the exercises that are more difficult for you and work on them, as well as the ones that you are comfortable doing.

Warming up

Given the intensity of squash, it is important to warm up before you start a game. Light running or bouncing on the spot are simple and effective ways of warming up. Look for the exercises that are good for you and repeat them before you start your matches every time . Creating this habit can also help to prepare you psychologically for your match. It's almost like a warning to your body and mind that it is time to get serious because there is some hard work coming.

A little bit about me

I'm originally from Hamilton, New Zealand. I grew up in squash surrounded by extremely talented players. It was an exceptional period for squash in New Zealand, during which the country produced world-class players like Bruce Brownlee, Murray Lilley, Ross Norman, Stuart Davenport, Susan Devoy, Robyn Blackwood and Joanne Williams.

The only full time squash coach in New Zealand at that time was the country's national coach, Dardir El Bakary, an Egyptian national and former world number three. I was always impressed by his passion for squash and especially his focus on how and where you should hit the ball.

When you started playing squash in those days, you were shown how to hold and move the racket, the basic shots and that was about it. We learnt by watching and imitating the better players. Those players would sometimes give advice on things we could improve or work on.

If you became one of the better players for your age group, you got a couple of days coaching during the season from the regional coach, who often gave up their own time on a voluntary basis.

You improved your squash by collecting new ideas from wherever you could and experimented with them. Some things helped and others you left behind.

I was introduced to squash when my parents joined the Cambridge Squash Club when I was eight or nine years old. We used to go onto any spare courts while our parents were in the club's bar after a tournament. I wasn't allowed to play regularly until I was twelve as my parents insisted that I play a team sport before starting an individual sport like squash. I had been playing rugby since I was eight years old.

By the time I was 14, I was biking the 2.5 kilometres most days to the Marist Squash Club to play against friends and club members. At 16 I decided to stop playing rugby and focus on squash. I played in my first national tournament, losing three of my four matches. But I had a great time!

When I was 17 and 18 I represented my district, Waikato, in the national under-19 team championships.

I started working in the Inland Revenue Department when I was 18. The flexible working hours of the government department allowed me to train twice a day, either early in the morning, or at lunchtime, and then every evening. Most weekends between April and October were occupied playing in different tournaments around the country. The few weekends without tournaments were used for training. On those weekends off I would sometimes hitchhike the 60 kilometres from Hamilton to Matamata (now famous for the hobbit village in the Lord of the Rings movies) to have a game with Andy Lusty. He was an Englishman who had been in the top ten in Britain. He had a unique and creative way of playing squash, constantly using all possible angles and walls of the court. His experience and level of play meant that I would sometimes come away with new concepts or ideas to work on.

When I was 19, I decided that a future in the Inland Revenue Department was not for me. I decided to go to England and use my squash as a way to travel around and visit Europe. To finance this adventure I needed to earn a lot more money so went to work for two summer seasons in the meat works, where they kill the cattle and sheep that New Zealand is so famous for. Work started at 5.15 am and I had to leave home at around 4.30am to bike the 18 kilometres from Hamilton to Horotiu. After work I biked to the Hamilton Squash club to do my daily training.

Andy had told me about the squash tours he had organised with other English players to Europe, Africa, Canada, Australia and New Zealand. His team was called the Churchillians.

This seemed like a great way to travel so four friends, who were all good squash players (Tony Brettkelly, Ray Lindsay, Anthony McMurtrie and Phil Wallace), and myself gave our team the name "The Young Kiwis". This was when I became a squash tourist. I wrote letters (no internet or email in those days) to all the national squash federations in Europe and most of the regional federations in Britain introducing The Young Kiwis and asking them if they were able to organise matches for our team. The replies allowed us to organise a four-week tour of Wales and England, combining playing team matches against different counties and clubs and competing in a couple of tournaments. The Irish Squash Association also replied, giving us a bus pass for two weeks, and organising matches against different counties around the country, including an open tournament at the Belfast Boat Club.

We then managed a couple of weeks in Sweden and Finland, coinciding with their open tournaments.

The World Teams Championship was in New Zealand that year, 1983, and I was selected in a New Zealand under-23 team that replaced a country that had withdrawn from the teams tournament. This allowed us to meet players from different countries and we arranged to visit Scotland between our travels around England, Wales and Ireland to train with players from their national team.

After the "tour" I stayed in London to train over the summer. I worked part-time in the squash club bar to survive economically.

I wanted to live in a non-English speaking environment and using squash seemed to the best option I had. I met a Belgian coach, Luc Raymacker, at the squash club in London. He offered to introduce me to clubs in Belgium. In June I visited him in Antwerp and visited various clubs. I got a job coaching at the Fort Jaco Squash Club in Brussels.

I returned to London and continued training. In September 1984 I went to Brussels to start work as a squash coach and learn French. David Norman, a friend and good squash player, joined me in Brussels, starting a coaching job at another club.

I wanted to play in as many tournaments as possible, but it wasn't easy finding information about them in the days before the internet. I heard about a tournament in Luxembourg and managed to enter. I arrived there ready to play on the Friday evening only to find that I had been removed from the draw because a well-known player had called on the Friday morning asking to play! No one knew who I was so they so they kicked me out and "forgot" to let me know. Fortunately I met the Australian, Frank Donnelly (former world amateur n° two), who helped me out. After Frank insisted, they let me play in the first round losers event. I didn't care, I just wanted to play. Frank also explained to me how the tournaments worked in the different countries and how to get information about them.

From then on, I managed to play in a tournament almost every weekend until the end of the season. I found tournaments in France, Switzerland, Holland, Germany and, of course, Belgium. I even won a few.

After the season in Europe I returned to New Zealand in April 1985 to play the season there and continued playing tournaments almost every weekend and league matches during the week. I finished the season in the top ten players in the country.

I returned to Brussels in September 1985 with Ray Lindsay and another friend from New Zealand, Dean Lovett. I started a new coaching job at the Castle Club and continued playing tournaments around Europe. In 1986 I joined PSA and managed to play five ranking tournaments and got a world ranking in the sixties. An English friend, David Atchinson, suggested trying life in Paris and helped us find coaching jobs there. Dean and I moved to Paris that summer where we continued to combine playing in tournaments and coaching.

In the spring of 1987 while doing some solo training I saw the relationship between the shoulder of my racket arm and the point of impact of the racket with the ball. I realised that if I had my racket prepared and could move my body to a position so that the ball was perpendicular to my shoulder it would go where I wanted it to almost every time. I also started to understand the reasons why the ball had not gone to where I wanted it to. This understanding is what I have tried to explain in this book.

Around the same time, Stuart Davenport and Jan Ulf Soderberg arranged a new coaching job for me in Barcelona at Can Melich Club and I started in September 1987. Can Melich Club had an exceptional team and squash school and during the three years I worked there our players won 36 Catalan and Spanish titles in the different categories, from under eleven years old through to the senior level. We also won four Spanish national teams titles.

In 1990 I decided to try my hand at another line of work and stopped working fulltime in squash.

However, I continued to coach Oriol Salvia and Elizabeth Sadó. Oriol was Spanish Champion twice, Catalan Champion twelve times and spent five years inside the top 100 PSA ranking. Elizabeth won the British Open under-19 title, was Spanish Champion seven times and Catalan Champion ten times.

I was also the Spanish national coach for two years which gave me the opportunity to work with an exceptional group of Spanish players, both on and off the court.

During my time as a squash tourist I played against many excellent and world-class players. I was also fortunate enough to play against, and/or train with, five world champions: Geoff Hunt, Ross Norman, Jahangir Khan, Jansher Khan and Susan Devoy.

The ideas in this book have come from a constant and ongoing learning process that seems to have no end. It is the result of collecting ideas from many different people over the years, playing and watching hundreds of games of squash, and trying to understand and put together the many different details that make up squash.

In the end, playing squash, like any sport or profession, is about how we are able to understand ourselves, our bodies, our minds, and how to develop each part to create habits which allow us to get to the G Spot consistently.

I hope that you find something that may be useful for your game in this collection of ideas.

Acknowledgements

Firstly I would like to thank Ignasi Herms, the director of the Catalan Squash Federation and the Catalan Squash Federation who remembered that he had an old guy living close by who used to play and coach squash and asked me to help them. Without his iniciative I would not have written this collection of ideas.

Dani Pascual for deciding to train with me. Giving me the chance to refesh my memory and presenting me with new coaching challenges.

Oriol Salvia whose limitless pasión for squash over the years kept me in touch with our sport even when life seemed to be pulling me in a different direction.

Elizabet Sadó whose ability to assimilate and put into practice new ideas always impressed me.

All the people who I have played and coached over the years, you have all contributed to my own learning process that has allowed me put together these ideas about squash.

My sisters, Joanne for doing the first proof reading and showing me how rusty my written english was. Tracy for organising the definitive proof reading and Lisa Robinson for doing it.

Simon my nephew the lawyer, who helped with the corrections, said after his first look at the book "I had thought it might be OK, but I didn't expect it to be that good, no offence intended".

Mireia Lopez, my business partner for helping to awake my interest in the written word, though our years of hunting for the right way to prepare our simple marketing texts.

Caitriona O'Leary for adding the Art to my texts.

Toni Ricart (Multistudio), who has magically put this collection of texts and sketches together in a book format.

Ortrud Lindeman, my Homeopathic doctor and Ferran Trindad my Osteopath. For keeping my body together going though the challenges that life sends and specially showing me that things are often not quite as simple as they seem, but if you take time to understand how the small details are interelated one can often find the real solutions. Two people who have found the G Spots in their professions.

Testimonials

"Some years ago Tony talked to me about writing a book. I am very happy that he has finally managed to do it and share his fasinating visión of our sport. He is a master at analizing the many aspects that make up squash. This is a great opportunity for all those who love playing squash to gain a deeper understanding of the game and define areas in which they can improve."

Elisabet Sadó Garriga
Former British Open under 14, 16 and 19 Champion,
7 times Spanish Champion and 10 times Catalan Champion.

"Tony is a wise man of our sport. He has a natural and instinctive way of understanding squash that comes from years of playing in tournaments and coaching. His experience and personal approach has allowed him to become an excellent coach. Many of my achievements are thanks to the way he is able to adapt his knowledge to each individual player. I am very happy that he has decided to share some of his "know how" in this book."

Oriol Salvia Corcoll
12 times Catalan Champion,
2 Times Spanish Champion and winner of 2 PSA Tournaments.

"What a fantastic resource for coaches and players alike. This comprehensive guide is a must for those who wishing to give squash enthusiasts the fundamentals of the game. Like anything mastering techniques and having a good understanding of all the facets of playing squash will not only improve your game but give you so much more enjoyment . I commend Tony on his ability to bring this all together."

Dame Susan Devoy
Winner of 8 British Open and 4 World Open Titles

"Tony Griffin takes us with him on a personal journey of enquiry into key squash ideas. These he explains, follow from his concept of the G-Spot. He takes a fresh look at familiar topics and investigates what factors affect the optimal hitting experience. The question Tony poses is, 'how to make this both natural and effective?' His ideas, experiences and influences come together into an important work which will challenge inquisitive players and thoughtful coaches to rethink some familiar concepts.

While the G-spot is all pervasive in many of the discussions, Tony also throws in advice and innovative methods on such things as how to maximise the chances of 'lucky' back corner nicks and the elimination of 'free shots´.

An interesting journey, challenging analysis and entertaining anecdotes make it a timely addition to squash instructional writing."

Ian Mckenzie
Editor, *The Squash Player magazine*

"Writing a coaching manual on any sport is difficult. Tony has succeeded brilliantly here by writing clear, easy to understand descriptions of how to learn to play and develop all the basic shots played in squash. His book importantly includes pairs routines, mental fitness, exercises, warm up routines and stretching, making it a complete coaching manual. The illustrations are a great addition. They capture in detail exactly what Tony is explaining. The catchy title lends itself very well to the way the book has been refreshingly written."

Ross Norman
Former World Champion.

"I have always believed that squash is about where and how you hit the squash ball. Tony's book explains this simply and clearly. He also talks about some of the finer points of squash that many players do instinctively without really understanding the full reasons behind them. I love the fact that the title of a book about squash can put a smile on people's faces."

Stuart Davenport
Former World n° 3

" This a great book for all levels . Nice anecdotes and a good technical focus with lots of insights . A good read with a different twist from other squash books."

Liz Irving
Former World n° 2
and coach of 7 times World Champion Nicol David

24924817R00067

Made in the USA
Middletown, DE
10 October 2015